To the Sisters of Charity
with my love
Sister Genevon McBride

The Bird Tail

THE BIRD TAIL

Sister Genevieve McBride, O.S.U.

Vantage Press
New York / Washington / Atlanta
Los Angeles / Chicago

130381

FIRST EDITION
Second Printing 1984

Published by Vantage Press, Inc.
516 West 34th Street, New York, New York 10001

Manufactured in the United States of America
ISBN: 533-01042-X

To my
Father and Mother,
Patrick and Mary McBride,
pioneers who loved
God and Montana,
to my sister, Regina,
Mother Clotilde Angela, who
paved the way with
Ursulines of the West,
and to my brother Jim

CONTENTS

ACKNOWLEDGMENT

THIS book is the simple story of a group of devoted missionaries who tried to help the Indians and whites in the early wilderness of Montana. It does not try to prove anything. Much of the material is recorded for the first time from letters, diaries, and annals.

It is impossible to list all to whom I am indebted for help on this project but I should like to mention a few. I am grateful to Most Reverend Eldon B. Schuster for his interest and encouragement, to Monsignor Francis Saksa for the use of the baptismal and marriage records of St. Peter's Mission, to Father Wilfred Schoenberg, S.J., for his help in the Archives of the Oregon Province of the Jesuits at Gonzaga University; to Mother Dolores Helbing, Provincial of the Western Province of the Ursulines, to Sister Marietta Devine and my community of Great Falls for their encouragement and help and to our dear Toledo Ursulines whose charity still follows us in Montana. I appreciate the help of Honorable Senator Mike Mansfield and his secretary, Mrs. Peggy Connelly De Michele, who have assisted me in many ways. There are all those in the various libraries where I have worked who have shown courtesy and encouragement, especially the succession of librarians at the Montana Historical Library in Helena; Miss Anna McDonnell, Miss Virginia Walton, Miss Mary Dempsey and the present librarian, Mrs. Harriet Meloy. I am indebted to my relatives who have made extra travel and research possible, Mary, Katherine, Julia, Madeliene, and Betty McAndrew. I am not unmindful of those dear friends, Margueritte Flaherty, May Brennan, Mrs. D.P. Conry, Beatrice Conry, Leonida Hagan, John and Mary Connelly Sullivan who have helped in so many ways. Mary Connelly Sullivan was one of the early students at St. Peter's and always a loyal friend. I should not omit those descendants of the first pupils at St. Peter's

Mission, Loretta and Walter Lemire, Elizabeth Chambers and Rosemary Kologi Siemens, Mary Pierre, Mable Mannix Pings, and Margaret Moran Halvorson, and Joe Moran whose father was the first great friend of the Ursulines and Jesuits. I am grateful to Helen Power for her encouragement and help, to Sister Marion McCrickard, Sister Jean Marie Wilkins and Pat Traub who spent many hours typing the manuscript. I owe the most to my dear sister, Mother Clotilde Angela, for her constant help, suggestions and inspiration.

December 10, 1972

MARY GENEVIEVE MCBRIDE, O.S.U.

INTRODUCTION

THE old Mullan Road from Fort Benton to the mines follows the Sun River for ten miles from the "Leavings," then crosses by a landmark known to all early trappers and travelers as the Bird Tail. It can be seen from miles—a huge promontory flanking the pass like some mythical bird with tail spread, an eternal phoenix. It has looked down over an endless pageant. The Indians on the way to the buffalo hunt prayed to this strange form and made their sacrificial offering of beads, weapons and cherished objects. The Blackfoot war parties passed and looked for help to the gigantic bird. The explorer, Meriwether Lewis, returning from the Columbia over the mountains, passed a few miles to the north down Sun River. The trapper headed for the mountains over this trail. The gold seeker hurried to the mines, knowing they were not far distant. The troops under General Gibbons passed by on their way to the battle with the Sioux. The early settlers brought their families and household goods up the same trail; the grave of a small child on the slope testified to this. The missionary bumped along in an old wooden wagon, saw the landmark and knew he was near home.

It was here, east of the Bird Tail, that the story of St. Peter's was written.

CHAPTER 1

Early Missionary Contacts with the Blackfoot

THE Blackfoot are members of the great Algonquin linguistic group. The three divisions — Piegan, Blood and Blackfoot groups — inhabit the region of the Rocky Mountains extending north far into Canada and south to the Missouri and at one time to the Tetons.[1]

Father Peter Prando, S.J., who lived among these Indians for many years, explains the name origins:

> The Indian name of the Blackfeet is *Siksikama*, that means black moccasin because by walking in the prairie when the fire burned great extensions of country their moccasins got black so they got their name.
>
> The name of the Blood Indians is *Kaenna* because they were fond of raw meat, and by eating it they were making their lips bloody. So the Indian sign for Blood Indians is to put the index of the right hand all along the lips on the top of them.
>
> The Piegan Indians give the following explanation: *Pikaniki* means buffalo robes not well tanned. It originated long ago on account of the laziness of the women or for want of their skill some men were going around with Buffalo robes not well dressed; and other people making fun of them gave these people such a name.[2]

The Jesuit Missionaries came to the Rocky Mountains at the request of the Flatheads. After establishing St. Mary's Mission in the Bitterroot and a center at St. Paul's on the Willamette, the missions spread throughout the Northwest

1

and California. The story is often told of the several requests for missionaries made by four different delegations to St. Louis from the Flathead tribe. Fortunately, the last delegation contacted Father De Smet who enthusiastically offered himself for the work. After a remarkable journey in the company of the American Fur Company, the missionary met the future Christians in the vicinity of Jackson's Hole and spent the month of July and part of August 1840 traveling with them through southern Idaho and Montana, instructing and baptizing them. When Father De Smet parted from the Flatheads, they expressed fear of his safety through the Yellowstone country and gave him an escort lest he fall into the hands of the Blackfoot.[3]

Father Christian Hoecken was in actuality the first Catholic priest to visit and administer the sacrament of Baptism in the region of Montana.

Christian Hoecken sailed from Antwerp on September 5, 1832, for the United States, his destination being the Jesuit novitiate in Maryland. From there he went to the new novitiate at Florissant, Missouri, on October 9, 1833.

In 1837, Father Hoecken was superior of the Kickapoo mission, and in 1838, he was among the Potawatomi Indians, the Sugar Creek Mission near present Centerville, Kansas. He was taken suddenly ill in July, 1839, and was recalled to the novitiate at Florissant.

When Father De Smet left Council Bluffs for St. Louis in February of 1840, Father Christian Hoecken replaced him. That same year Father Hoecken made his historic trip up the Missouri to Fort Union. He no doubt traveled on the *Trapper* which arrived June 27. Larpenteur, who traveled on the boat, states that it arrived at Fort Union on that date.[4] It is known that Father Hoecken baptized the following at Fort Union:[5]

On June 28, 1840:
Elizabeth, daughter of Mr. Robert and an Indian.
Julie, daughter of Indians, 5 years.
Robert, son of Mr. Edward Denig and an Indian, 5 years.
Jean Baptista, son of Mr. Michael Champagne and an

Indian, 5 years.

Josette, daughter of Mr. Michael Champagne and an Indian, 18 months.[6]

Joseph, son of Mr. Bonaventure le Brun and an Indian, 4 years, born Feb. 10, 1836.

Marie, daughter of the same, born Dec. 12, 1838.
On June 29:

Henrietta, daughter of Mr. Josette, 6 years.

Father Hoecken returned to Council Bluffs and St. Louis. In 1852, he accompanied Father De Smet on one of his missionary trips up the Missouri and died in the service of the sick on board.

Letter to Editor of the *Précis Historique*, Brussels
University of St. Louis, Jan. 16, 1852
On the 7th of last June (June 7, 1851) boat to go to Fort Union. Members of American Fur Co. on board 80 men. Accompanied by Father Christian Hoecken I embarked at this place (St. Louis) on board steamer *St. Ange* to go to the Rocky Mountains.

The inundations of the river, the continued rains of spring and the sudden transition from heat to cold are in this climate, sure precursors of malignant fevers. The cholera appears to assume an epidemic type in these regions. . .We were 500 miles from St. Louis when the cholera broke out in the steamer. . .A bilious attack confined me to my bed nearly ten days. . .Good Father Hoecken devoted himself to the sick night and day, with a zeal at once heroic and indefatigable. He visited them; he assisted them in their sufferings; he prepared and administered remedies; he rubbed the cholera patients with camphor; he heard the confessions of the dying, and lavished upon them the consolations of religion. He then went and blessed their graves on the banks of the river, and buried them with the prayers and ceremonies prescribed by the Roman ritual.[7] Father Hoecken's cabin was next to mine. Between one and two o'clock at night, when all on board was calm and quiet, and the sick in their wakefulness heard naught but the sighs and moans of their fellow sufferers, the voice of Father Hoecken was suddenly heard. He was calling me to his assistance. Awakening from a deep sleep, I recognized his voice and dragged myself to his pillow. Ah me! I found him ill and even in extremity. He asked me to hear his confession; I at once acquiesced in his desire. Dr. Evans, a physician of great experience and of remarkable charity, endeavored to relieve him, and watched by him, but his cares and remedies proved fruitless. . .Father Hoecken, ripe for heaven, surrendered his pure soul into the hands of his Divine Redeemer on the 19th of June, 1851, twelve days after our departure from St. Louis.[8] A decent coffin, very thick and tarred within, was prepared to receive his mortal remains; a temporary grave was dug in a beautiful forest in the vicinity of the mouth of the Little Sioux, and the burial was performed with all the ceremonies of the Church, in the evening of the 19th of June, all on board assisting. About a month later, on the return of the *St. Ange* which passed our venerated tomb, the coffin was exhumed, put on board the boat and transported to the Novitiate of the Society of Jesus at Florissant.[9]

Father Hoecken had been a devoted missionary. An Indian pupil of St. Mary's among the Potawatomi, Joseph Moore, describes his activities:

Without interfering with the duties of his mission and his duties to God, he was among the Indians in their sports and hunts; and in the spring, when the Indians helped one another to plant corn, the most industrious figure in the crowd was the Jesuit Father with a large plantation hoe, an apron sack full of corn, and a big Dutch pipe in his mouth. He came, indeed, to teach the Indians civilization. He owned one yoke of oxen, poorly kept going the rounds from one family to another to do the breaking. It is said that he was charitable to an excessive degree. Being in

4

the company of Indians so much, he spoke their language with the fluent ease of a native.[10]

Father Verrey, one of his companions at Council Bluffs, Sugar Creek, and St. Mary's, wrote of him:

He was truly a zealous father, constantly occupied from morning until night with the spiritual and temporal welfare of the Indians. The sick were never neglected by him. It appeared to have been his glory to attend the sick, not only as a doctor for the maladies of his soul, but as a physician for the body.[11]

In 1841 Father De Smet returned to the Rocky Mountains to establish St. Mary's Mission in the Bitterroot Valley. He brought with him five companions: Father Nicholas Point, Father Gregory Mengarine, Brother William Claessens, Brother Joseph Specht and Brother Charles Huet. Two of these, Father Point and Brother Claessens, were destined to labor for the conversion of the Blackfoot.

One of the most perilous journeys of the indefatigable missionary was that undertaken to find this tribe and convert them. The neighboring tribes had a respectful fear of them and had engaged periodically in quarrels with them and even bloodshed. Father De Smet left the St. Ignatius establishment in August, 1845, to reach them from the West. He arrived at Rocky Mountain House on October 4, without seeing any of them. A few days after his arrival a few came to the post. He pushed eastward over the mountains as far as Fort Edmonton, where he met the Oblate Missionaries, October 30, 1845. In order to be able to make the trip on snowshoes he underwent a fast to reduce his weight. It was March, 1846, before he was able to make the return trip, disappointed at the failure of his mission.[12]

Father De Smet and Father Point[13] left St. Mary's Mission in August, 1845, traveled with the Indians to the buffalo hunt and then on to Fort Lewis on the Missouri. Old Nicholas, whom Father De Smet speaks of as his first Blackfoot convert, was happy to bring the Blackrobe to his people. An unfortunate accident occurred; a fall from his horse was fatal and Nicholas died not too far distant from the post. Fort Lewis at this time was in charge of Major Culbertson who had established the trading post on the Missouri a few miles above the present site of Fort Benton.[14]

Father Point was regarded with esteem by Major Culbertson although they did not always agree. He was furnished quarters at the Fort with a room for chapel and school. Lieutenant Bradley speaks of him as a man of great austerity and severe in the practice of his religion. He reproved profanity and immorality and was feared and respected by all in the Fort.

On one occasion when Culbertson's child was ill with croup, the Indian mother admitted an old Blood medicine woman. When Father Point sat down to breakfast with Major Culbertson, he heard the weird strain of the Indian woman's "incantations." He left his breakfast, and went upstairs and unceremoniously ejected the medicine woman. He then reprimanded the Major for permitting such pagan practices.[15]

Father Point said he did not waste his time at the Fort. He wrote:

> I have performed six hundred and sixty-seven baptisms, the records of which are in due form; I have taken notes of whatsoever appeared to me suitable for interesting the curious or edifying the pious. During the winter I was accustomed daily to give three instructions, or catechetical lessons, proportioned to the three very different classes of my auditors. It is unnecessary for me to say that the prayers have all been translated into Blackfoot, and learned in Fort Louis and in the camp of the Piegans, and there is scarcely any camp among the Blackfeet in which the sign of the cross is not held in veneration, and even practised at least among those individuals who have had any intercourse with the missionary.[16]

Father Point left in May for St. Louis enroute to Canada where he was assigned to future work in the Society. When he left Fort Lewis, the post was being transferred down the river to its present site. He speaks of stopping at the new post which he calls Fort Clay. However, the post continued to be known as Fort Lewis until the name was changed by Culbertson in 1850 to Fort Benton in honor of Senator Benton.[17]

Father Adrian Hoecken wrote in April, 1847, to Father De Smet that Father Menetrey had gone to Fort Benton in the fall and had stayed some time waiting for the boats. He speaks with high praise of the Blackfoot and regrets his lack of jurisdiction over them.[18] In another letter he again urges the establishment of a mission among them even if the death of a martyr be necessary to bring the hundredfold.[19]

Governor Stevens, during August and September, 1855, collected the various tribes for the Blackfoot Council which was held at the mouth of the Judith. The plan to change the site for the Council was necessitated because of the difficulty in getting the supplies for the Indians beyond that point. The Council opened on October 16 and the treaty was signed on October 17. By the terms of this treaty the Blackfoot were to be free to hunt the buffalo north of the Missouri but the territory between the Yellowstone and the Missouri was to be common hunting ground for all the tribes. Schools, farms and annuities were promised them.[20]

Father Hoecken accompanied by Father Croke went to the Council with the Flatheads. Father Croke baptized several at Fort Benton, signing himself "Traveling Oregon Missionary."[21] Father Hoecken wrote to Father De Smet from the Flathead Camp in the country of the Blackfoot, urging the establishment of a mission among them.[22]

[1] Clark Wissler, *The American Indian* (New York: Yale University Press, 1938) p. 39.

[2] Rev. Peter Prando, S.J., (Ms.) *Notes,* Lindesmith Collection, Museum Catholic University, Washington, D.C.

[3] Hiram Chittenden, and Alfred Richardson, *Life, Letters and Travels of Father Pierre-Jean De Smet, 1801-1873,* vol. 1 (New York: Francis P. Harper, 1905), pp. 198-244.

[4] Larpenteur, *Forty Years a Fur Trader.* 2 Vols. N.Y., 1898. Vol. 1, p. 161.

[5] Hoecken, Christian, *Baptismal Record.* St. Mary's College, St. Mary's, Kansas.

[6] Nicholas Point, S.J., *Wilderness Kingdom*, Indian Life in the Rocky Mountains, 1840-1847, The Journals and Paintings of Nicholas Point, S.J., Translated and introduced by Joseph P. Donnelly, S.J. (New York: Holt, Rinehart and Winston, 1967).

[7] De Smet, J. J., *Western Missions and Missionaries: A Series of Letters*, New York, 1859, pp. 61-64.

[8] Ibid. pp. 61-63.

[9] Ibid. p. 64.

[10] Garraghan, *Jesuits in the Middle United States*, vol. 2, p. 630.

[11] *Ibid.*, p. 630.

[12] Hiram Chittenden and Alfred Richardson, *Op. cit.*, vol. 2, pp. 484-551.

[13] Father Nicholas Point was a native of La Vendée and had been president of the first Jesuit College in Louisiana which was later moved to New Orleans and became Loyola University. He was an enigma to his fellow workers but a soul filled with zeal for the conversion of the Indians. He founded Sacred Heart Mission at Coeur d'Alene in 1842.

[14] Fort Piegan was temporarily established in October, 1831, between the Missouri and the Marias for trade with the Blackfoot. In 1832 Fort MacKenzie was established near the mouth of the Marias. This fort was burned and replaced by Fort Lewis, a site farther up the river, in 1844. Rev. James Stuart, "Adventures on the Upper Missouri," *Montana Historical Contributions*, vol. 1, 2nd ed. Montana Independent Pub. Co., 1902, p. 76.

[15] Lieut. J. W. Bradley, "Affairs at Fort Benton," *Historical Society of Montana Contributions*, Helena, vol. 1, pp. 248,249.

[16] Rev. P.J. De Smet, S.J., *Western Missions* (New York: P.J. Kenedy, 1859) p. 250.

[17] The old site of Fort Lewis was unfavorable because of the floating ice in the spring, which prevented the Indians crossing the river. The old fort was taken down and the timbers rafted to the new site. Ref. Lieut. J. W. Bradley, *Op. cit.* p. 251.

[18] Rev. P. J. De Smet, S.J., *Western Missions*, *Op. cit.*, p. 311.

[19] *Ibid.*, p. 317.

[20] Hazard Stevens, *Life of General Isaac I. Stevens*, 2 vols. (Boston and New York: Houghton, Mifflin & Co., 1900) vol. 2, pp. 111-115.

[21] *Baptismal Register* of St. Peter's, now in Chancery Office, Great Falls, Montana.

[22] Letter of Father Hoecken to Father De Smet in *Cinquante Nouvelles Lettres du R. P. De Smet*, Paris, 1858, pp. 287, 288.

CHAPTER 2

The Blackfoot Mission Established

ON September 10, 1858, Alfred Vaughan, the agent for the Blackfoot, wrote in his report to Washington that he had selected a site for the government farm. He examined the regions around the Highwood, the Missouri and Sun Rivers. He was accompanied up the Sun River by Father Congiato and Father Hoecken and Major Owen, who at that time was Agent for the Flatheads. The advantages of the valley of Sun River decided the location of the farm. Mr. Vaughan contracted for the erection of the necessary buildings and enclosures for stock. The Jesuits assured him that a school for the Indians would be established in the spring.[1]

In the fall of 1859 Father Hoecken selected a site on the Teton about 75 miles from Fort Benton, where small cabins were erected. Father Hoecken was joined by Father Imoda in October, 1859.[2] The site was near the landmark, Priest's Butte, just south of the present town of Choteau.

In the spring of 1860, the location was changed to the south bank of Sun River, about eight miles above the site of Fort Shaw. Father Giorda says this change was made because of the lack of wood. After a few months Father Hoecken was changed and left for the East so the site was abandoned and the Fathers moved to the old trading post of Fort Campbell near Fort Benton. Father Imoda and Father Giorda lived here, and were later joined by Father Menetrey in October, 1861.[3]

In May, 1862, Father De Smet left St. Louis on the *Spread Eagle*, taking six weeks for the journey. He was met by Father Giorda and Father Imoda, and two coadjutor Brothers who were settled among the Blackfoot. He supplied the missionaries with church ornaments, sacred vessels, food, clothing, tools, an ambulance and wagon. Father De Smet describes his visit:

> I offered the Holy Sacrifice of the Mass among them by way of thanksgiving. An Indian choir, composed of men and women, young men and girls, chanted the litanies of the Holy Virgin and songs to the glory of God and our Lord Jesus Christ and in praise of his good Mother, "whom all nations called blessed." Everything was sung in the language of the country. A goodly number drew devoutly near to the holy table.[4]

The site decided upon for a new location of St. Peter's, according to Father Cataldo's account, was to be at Willow Round on the Marias River. Temporary trading posts had been established here at different times and it was a favorite landmark and gathering place for the Indians. Father De Smet left for St. Louis on July 6, and on July 10 the loaded wagons were ready to start for the new Mission site, but were delayed.

On July 17 news was received that at Willow Round there was a disturbance. Crows stole horses belonging to whites and Piegans, and one Piegan was killed. It was decided not to settle there so "that was the last of Willow Round."[5]

Father De Smet on his recent visit brought word that Father Giorda had been appointed General Superior of the Missions on January 21.

Since Father Giorda was in charge, it was his task to find another site for the mission. He decided on one on the Missouri River on land that formed a peninsula because of a great bend in the river just opposite Smith River or Deep Creek. It is known to a few old timers today as Churchill Bend and is just one mile south of the present Ulm on the Great Northern. Here in February, 1863, the Mission began; Father Giorda nearly lost his life shortly after. He tried to cross the river on the ice and fell in and would have been lost had not a Blackfoot lassoed him and hauled him to the shore. Father was so grateful for the rescue that he made a vow to spend the rest of his life as a missionary with these Indians.

Circumstances, however, prevented.

Several cabins were built at the foot of a hilly ridge that shut off the Mission from view of the prairie beyond. The missionaries had difficulties of various kinds. One year the crops were scanty and the river overflowed,[6] and the Indians were unfriendly, instigated by trouble with the whites.[7]

In May of that year, Father De Smet, accompanied by two Italian Brothers, left to visit the Mission established on the Missouri. The river was so low that the boat was not able to come farther than the mouth of the Milk River where they stayed for four weeks. Wagons were sent from Fort Benton to transport the freight from the steamer. A comfortable conveyance was dispatched by the Fathers for the use of Father De Smet and the two Brothers. [8] Father De Smet writes:

> We arrived at Fort Benton on the day of the glorious Assumption of the Holy Virgin. There, I had the consolation of meeting Father Imoda of the Mission of St. Peter who had come thither to see me. We tarried here several days, to recover from our fatigue as well as to instruct and baptize a goodly number of Crow or Absoraka children. They reached the fort at about the same time as ourselves, having come to exchange their peltries for such things as they needed. The Mission of St. Peter is situated on the Missouri ten miles above the Great Falls, and seventy-five miles from Benton.[9]

On the 25th of August, Father De Smet left St. Peter's for St. Ignatius[10] and returned to St. Louis by way of Fort Vancouver and the Isthmus of Panama.

A false rumor of the discovery of gold at Sun River brought a stampede to the settlement about twenty miles from the Mission. The thermometer was 34 degrees below zero. This mad mob of crazed gold seekers rushed into the region where there was neither food nor shelter sufficient to protect them. Many drifted into the mission, some with frozen feet and hands. Fortunately, the skill of Father Ravalli

11

saved some from death and amputated limbs.[11]

On December 26, 1863, Father Giorda left Fort Benton on a missionary trip with the Piegans. He camped on the Teton with some Indians belonging to Little Robe's Band. Fearing the Gros Ventres, whom they heard were in the neighborhood, they moved up the Teton. Here they encountered a group of whiskey traders who moved along with them to Big Lake's Camp and remained there for several days because of the storms. They moved on to the Marias but on the way were lost for two days on the prairie. When they arrived at the Piegan Camp on the Marias, whiskey traders from the mountains appeared. The poor missionary found the conditions intolerable. The Indians were soon crazed with drink and were in no mood to listen to the missionary. Father Giorda had started a school in two lodges, and three times a day taught the young boys, girls, women and some of the men their prayers and gave them religious instruction. Soon it became impossible to hold classes. Father Giorda wrote to Mr. Upson, the Blackfoot Indian Agent:

What will be the result of this whiskey trading and drinking among the Blackfeet? Of course they will grow the more poor, lazy and stupid. They will be brutalized. They will drink their robes, their homes; they will drink their daughters and their wives.[12]

Father Giorda did not claim to be a prophet but he foresaw what would happen if the whiskey trade continued. The Indians were trading their horses for whiskey. They needed horses to hunt the buffalo, so would be tempted to steal from the whites. This, in turn, would lead to war and destruction.[13]

Attempts were made in 1865 to find a more suitable spot for the Mission. Father Giorda, Father Kuppens, Father Imoda, Mr. Viel and a Blackfoot Indian guide set out in search of a more desirable location. After examining the land along the Dearborn and the Sun River, they decided on a valley east of the Bird Tail.

Father Kuppens described this familiar landmark:

Bird Tail is a very peculiar landmark near the Mullan road about midway between the Dearborn and Sun Rivers. It is a high, isolated and very steep hill, and the many large fragments of rock all about its sides give it a formidable aspect. The top appears to be one Solid Mass of Stones, and at its very highest point there juts out bold against the sky perhaps (seven) tall monoliths of colossal size. The Indians, in designating the hill, would raise their open hand above their head and extend the fingers. Very little effort of the imagination was required to find that the name Bird Tail was appropriate. Open hand, perhaps, would have done just as well, but the first white settlers called it "Bird tail, Bird tail!"[14]

This peaceful valley, reached by a cut-off from the Mullan road, is enclosed on one side by rugged peaks of the Big Belt Range, green with pine and fir, and on the other side with barren rocky hills of rugged shape. The traveler seeing it for the first time experiences delight and surprise at the sudden beauty of it all.

A camp was established here and work begun on the new buildings which were ready for occupancy by spring. During the winter General Thomas Francis Meagher, lost in a blizzard, found hospitality there.

In a letter to Father De Smet, Acting Governor Meagher describes his visit to the new site near the Bird Tail:

Executive Office, Virginia City
Dec. 15, 1865

My dear Father De Smet,

. . .I set out one day about the middle of last month for Benton from the new city of Helena. . .

A pleasant party of gentlemen set out with me. There was Judge Munson, and Associate-Judge of the United States District Court of Montana, Mr. Wood, Sheriff of Edgerton County of which Helena is the county seat, Mr. Hedges, a young lawyer. . . Mr. (Malcolm) Clark, formerly agent at Ft. Benton for the American Fur Company and one of the oldest residents of the territory. . .

You, my dear Father De Smet, are familiar with the reasons which determined the Fathers of the old mission to look out for a change of residence. The old mission, desirable in every other respect, is badly wanting in facilities for irrigation, and hence, the cattle which in the winter and early spring thrive so heartily there. . .in the summer and autumn suffer a good deal and fall off in flesh considerably. Owing to the same circumstances the Fathers find it impossible to raise anything like the quantity of grain and vegetables they require. . .we proposed to make our next halting place on our road to Benton. The mission I refer to here is the new mission of St. Peter's, so called since it was on the feast of St. Peter that Father Kuppens dedicated it to the missionary purposes of your generous and heroic Order. . .

. . .the barking of a robust old dog informed us that we were trespassers. . .and then Father Kuppens thrust his cheerful face out through the flap or apron which serves as the door of the Indian tent or tepee. . .

St. Peter's mission, at the moment I now speak of, consisted architecturally of an Indian tent or tepee capable of accommodating sixteen persons in Indian fashion, a wall tent as it is called in the army, which served as a storeroom, a grinding stone, and a commodious ambulance of rather an elegant air and finish, which formerly belonged to your good friend, General Harney, and which that splendid old soldier had, as you are aware, given to the Fathers. Behind these tents and this stylish ambulance rose the bold and picturesque hills. . .

The snow. . .detained us at St. Peter's for a day and a half, longer than we intended. . .

(Father Kuppens accompanied Meagher to the old St. Peter's Mission on the Missouri.)

When about halfway to the mission he (Father

14

Kuppens) told us of the narrow escape he had just there, a few months before, from the Piegans who rode down upon him suddenly, seized his bridle and insisted upon having his horse. Father Kuppens defended himself with his whip, struck the vermillioned rascals across the face a staggering blow — first one and then another and, rapidly taking advantage of the effect of his impetuous assault, had the satisfaction of leaving his importunate acquaintances half a mile behind him in a very short time. Not, however, before he received from the party compliment in a shower of arrows. . .one of which penetrating his thigh inflicted a rather severe wound.[15]

The position of the Fathers at the Mission became perilous. On April 22, 1866, a group of about thirty Indians (some thought they were led by Bull's Head) attacked the buildings at Sun River Government Farm. Cas Huff and Nicholas Shannon were then at the farm. Huff was killed while going from the house to the river for water. The Indians then set fire to the house. Shannon stayed inside until the heat fired off the loaded guns. When the flames reached some boxes of shells for a twelve pound howitzer, Shannon jumped from the window just before the shells exploded. The building timbers were hurled in all directions, completely demolishing the house. Shannon escaped, but took three days to reach a ranch on the Dearborn. The Indians killed seven head of oxen and moved on to the Mission on the Missouri. They killed the boy who was herding the cattle, James Fitzgerald, and slaughtered ten head of fine stock.[16]

Father Giorda describes the attack on the mission in a letter written to the Acting Governor, Thomas Francis Meagher, April 28, 1866, Helena, Montana Territory:

Excellent Governor: The most sad intelligence reached me just now from the Blackfoot Mission. Father Imoda and Father Ravalli sent me an expressman with letters to the effect that close to the old mission one of our men by the name of James Fitzgerald got shot and scalped by Indians while he was herding our stock. Father Ravalli, seeing that he was so long in coming in, sent the Indian boy, the remaining hand, to explore and the boy found poor James with four balls lodged in his back and a number of arrows in his breast. The Indians were driving away the stock. However, some few have been recovered. It is suspected that some five head have been slaughtered.

All the horses and cattle of Mr. Morgan are either stolen or butchered. Eighteen head of horses gone. Mr. Kennedy's band is partly stolen, partly butchered, and partly wounded. All the road to Benton from Clark's[17] down is lined with war parties.

I must leave today to go and see and perhaps remove the Mission and my brethren.

We would hope that as we were of necessity obliged by violence to retire for the moment that the property and claims of the mission and missionaries will be protected by law and secured.[18]

When Father Giorda arrived at the Mission it was decided the move should be made to the new location at once. However, after a short stop at the Bird Tail, it was thought best to move on over the mountains until the Indian unrest had subsided. During the removal, the missionaries met several groups of Indians and whites stirred up for trouble. The Fathers remained just one night at the new location and moved to St. Ignatius and Hell Gate, temporarily leaving the Mission.[19] Father Giorda stopped in Helena from May 8 until May 16, and then went on to Hell Gate.

After the Indian uprising, acting Governor General Francis Meagher organized a militia to protect the Mullan Road. The Government sent troops of soldiers who were quartered at the abandoned mission on the Missouri during that winter of 1866 and 1867. In the spring the new fort on Sun River was built and the troops transferred there. The post was called Fort Reynolds but it soon changed to Fort Shaw.[20]

Father De Smet went up the Missouri to Fort Benton in 1866 on the *Ontario* but was not able to visit the Missions. "I have not had the consolation of meeting the Fathers of the Mission of St. Peter's," he writes. "A fresh and furious war has broken out between the Whites and Blackfeet and our Fathers have been obliged to withdraw for the moment."[21]

Father Bougis wrote that Father Menetrey was sent to St. Peter's in 1868 but in 1869 he was replaced by Father Gazoli. Father Menetrey was at the Mission during the summer of 1868 when a traveler on horseback visited the Mission. The Mission comprised a farm of three hundred and twenty acres, partly enclosed and under cultivation. The mission farmer, Mr. Chote, raised wheat, barley and oats, and a garden of such vegetables as tomatoes, corn, asparagus, and melons. The buildings consisted of four or five large double cabins with extensive corrals sixteen or eighteen feet high.[22]

The Mission during these years was visited periodically by the Jesuit Fathers and remained under the care of Mr. Thomas Moran, an early settler in the valley and a faithful friend of the missionaries.[23]

The Mission was reopened in 1874 under the care of Father Imoda, with Brother Francis De Kock and Brother Lucien d'Agostino. Father Philip Rappagliosi came in July and labored among the Indians until his death on Milk River, February 7, 1878.[24] Father Imoda built a small log church and new cabins about a quarter of a mile from the first site. This was the year 1875. The altar was carved by Brother John and still adorns the little log church.

Father Damiani and Father Laltanzi of the Roman Province came to St. Peter's in 1879; Father Damiani in April and Father Laltanzi in December. In June, 1880, Father Laltanzi, because of his health, returned to Rome and was replaced by Father Peter Prando. A stone building was erected at this time and Father Damiani appointed superior.[25]

Father Prando states that, in the Christmas season, he had had the happiness of baptizing an Indian woman 120 years old, a medicine woman. She was his first Blackfoot convert

17

Left to right: Thomas Moran and Edward Lewis.

and he called her Mary. On New Year's Day he baptized a Blackfoot boy whom he named Joseph.

While at St. Peter's Mission, Father Prando ministered to the needs of the soldiers at Fort Shaw where he formed a Catholic Society. He speaks with appreciation of the Commander of the Fort who, although a Protestant, was courteous to the missionary and ordered a drumbeat to announce the time for Mass.[26]

At Sun River there was yet no church. Mass was held in the schoolhouse, which was also the dance hall. Father Prando preferred to use the old abandoned school instead.

The Jesuits from the Mission often offered Mass at the Fort, which is about fifteen miles away. The wife of Lieutenant Roe wrote interesting letters of life at this frontier army post. In one, dated January, 1879, she described an entertainment given for the Mission.

Our little entertainment for the benefit of the Mission here was a wonderful success. Every seat was occupied, every corner packed, and we were afraid that the old theatre might collapse. We made eighty dollars clear of all expenses.[27]

[1] Report of the Commissioner of Indian Affairs, Washington, 1855. The site of this government farm was on the north bank of Sun River, a short distance from the crossing at the present town of Sun River.

[2] Lieut. J. Bradley, *St. Peter's Mission* (Ms.), Montana State Historical Library, Helena. There are corrections and notes in the handwriting of Father Giorda which are a valuable source for this sketchy period.

[3] *Ibid.*

[4] Hiram Chittenden, and Alfred Richardson, *Op. cit.* pp. 785-787.

[5] Cataldo, S.J., *Memorabilia Giorda*, (Ms.) Jesuit Archives.

[6] Gad E. Upson, *Letter to Hon. W. P. Doli*, Indian Affairs (Ms.), Dept. of Interior, Washington, D.C.

Father Joseph Giorda, S.J.

[7] Rev. L. Palladino, S.J., *Indian and White in the Northwest* (Lancaster: Wickersham Publishing Co., 1922), pp. 205-207.

[8] Hiram Chittenden, and Alfred Richardson, *Op. cit.* pp. 792, 793.

[9] Ibid., pp. 793, 794.

[10] Ibid., 3: 795.

[11] Robert Vaughan. *Then and Now or Forty-Six Years in the Rockies*, Minneapolis Tribune, 1900, pp. 109, 110.

[12] Rev. J. Giorda (Ms.), Letter to Mr. Gad E. Upson, Archives, Dept. of Interior, Washington, D.C., Jan. 22, 1864.

[13] Ibid., This letter is cited and quoted by Howard Harrod in *Mission Among the Blackfeet* (Norman: U. of Oklahoma Press, 1971), pp. 56,57.

[14] F. X. Kuppens, S.J., *Notes on St. Peter's Mission* (Ms.), Jesuit Archives.

[15] *Irish Monthly*, Sept. 1902, vol. 14, p. 11

[16] Report of the Commissioner of Indian Affairs for the Year 1866, Washington, D.C., Government Printing Office, 1866, p. 203.

[17] Malcolm Clark's ranch was located at the head of Prickly Pear Canyon on the Mullan road.

[18] Letter signed "F. Giorda, S.J., Superintendent of the Indian Mission" in *The Montana Post*.

[19] Rev. L. Palladino, S.J., *Op. cit.*, pp. 206-209

[20] Lieutenant Gould Shaw at the head of a colored regiment lost his life in the Civil War. A magnificent monument by Augustus St. Gaudens stands in front of the State House on Boston Commons, a memorial to this valiant son of Massachusetts.

[21] Hiram Chittenden, and Alfred Richardson, *Op. cit.*, Vol. 3, p. 858.

[22] "Horseback Riders in Montana," *The Montana Post*, Friday, August 7, 1868, vols. 3, 4, Helena, Montana Historical Library.

[23] Rev. L. Palladino, S.J., *Op. cit.*, p. 211.

[24] *Ibid.*, p. 218. The life of Father Rappagliosi, S.J. was written in Italian.

[25] Bougis, S.J., *Sketch of the History of St. Peter's Mission*, pp. 8-11. (Ms.) Jesuit Archives.

[26] *Letter to Father Cataldo, St. Peter's Mission*, M.T. June 13, 1881. Woodstock Letters, vol. 12 (1881), pp. 145, 146.

[27] Roe, Frances M.A., *Army Letters from an Officer's Wife 1871-1888* (New York and London: D. Appleton & Co. 1909) p. 218.

CHAPTER 3

The Cheyenne Mission

WHEN the news of the Custer Massacre reached the outside world, the Ursulines of Toledo, Ohio, did not know that the bloody battle on the Little Big Horn would eventually bring about their missionary venture into Montana Territory. But so it came about.

The Northern Cheyennes had originally inhabited regions in Minnesota, but had been pushed westward by other tribes and the white settlers. They lived for a time in the region that is now North Dakota. Their history is one of brave defiance in the face of starvation and depredation of their hunting grounds.

This tribe had joined the Sioux in the attack on the Seventh Cavalry. They had more than one grievance against the U. S. Government. Driven out of the Black Hills, they had found fertile hunting grounds in the valleys of the Powder, Tongue and Rosebud Rivers. Once again they were ordered to move. Then followed one bloody encounter after another.

"After the Custer battle all the Indians moved up Little Sheep River and then over to Pole Creek (Clear Creek, a tributary of the Powder River). There they separated. The Sioux went west to the Tongue River and the Rosebud, and with them, about ten lodges of Cheyennes. . . .The other Cheyennes moved toward the Big Horn Mountains and then to the head of Powder River where General McKenzie found them.". . .This group later joined the Sioux near the site of the present St. Labre's Mission. "White Bull and Two Moons went up Tongue River; General Miles was following up Tongue River." Some of Miles' Crow scouts captured two of the women and boys. "In the spring one of the women was sent to the camp of the Cheyennes with a message from General Miles asking them to go to the fort and surrender. Two Moons, White Bull and others set out for the fort."[1]

General Miles himself states:

These Indians surrendered on good faith in the winter of 1877. The principal ones, Two Moons, White Bull, Horse Roads, Iron Shield, Brave Wolf with seven others, remained as hostages giving their persons as a guaranty for the good faith of the others. I gave them their choice to surrender there or at the agencies. Over five hundred surrendered on the Yellowstone and over three thousand at the agencies. Sitting Bull and his band fled to Canada, and Lame Deer's band took refuge in the broken country of the Rosebud, declaring that no white men could get near their camp, and defying the government.

After the surrender had been completed an expedition was organized against Lame Deer's band of sixty lodges, and called upon those that had surrendered to act as guides. White Bull, Two Moons and Hump rendered most valuable service on that expedition. The command surprised Lame Deer's camp, killing him and several of the principal warriors, capturing the entire camp and some 450 head of horses, mules, and ponies, and following them until they were finally driven into the agency. . . .There is no reason why Indians can not be well treated and allowed to live in peace in the vicinity in which they were born.[2]

After the Battle of the Little Big Horn, General Miles established a cantonment at the junction of the Tongue River and the Yellowstone. In July, 1877, a traveler wrote:

At the mouth of the Tongue River there is a large cantonment of troops stationed here to control the wandering band of Sioux that have given so much trouble during the last few years — the garrison came up from Fort Leavenworth on board a steamboat, their furniture being stored on a second vessel. Unfortunately, the boat on which the furniture was laden blew up.[3]

Near here Fort Keogh was constructed and the town of Miles grew up.[4] The town had grown large

24

enough to have a school. On October 6, school opened in a rented building on Old Road a few minutes walk from the Court House. The bell from the steamer *Yellowstone* was used.[5]

Reverend Eli Washington John Lindesmith was born September 7, 1827, and ordained a priest on July 8, 1885, for the Cleveland Diocese. He boasted that he was named for the greatest prophet of the Old Testament, the greatest of the New, and the Father of our country. His two great grand-uncles, George and Jacob, fought in the Revolution; his grand-uncles John and Peter fought in the War of 1812; and he had nineteen cousins who were Union soldiers in the Civil War.

Father Lindesmith was commissioned chaplain in the U.S. Army, July 1, 1880, and served until September 7, 1891. He was assigned to Fort Keogh, Montana Territory, and was sworn in July 2, 1880 at New Lisbon, Ohio. On July 22 he left Leitonia for Chicago, St. Paul, and Fort Snelling. On August 2, he left St. Paul on the Northern Pacific for Bismarck, North Dakota, and then took the steamer *Big Horn* up the Missouri to Fort Buford, thence by boat down the Yellowstone. The new chaplain arrived at Fort Keogh, August 11, 1880.

He was received with kindness by General Miles, and given temporary housing next to the Post Trading Store. After six weeks Father moved to comfortable quarters of six rooms in a double house. He gave his front room to Lt. H. J. Allan who lived there six months. The other half of the quarters was occupied by Lt. J. M. T. Partello and family. Lt. Partello later received a gold medal for being the best marksman in the American Army.

The chaplain set up his private chapel in one room where he said Mass on weekdays, heard confessions, baptized, taught catechism, and officiated at marriages. He dedicated his chapel to St. Ann.

A Post chapel was located in another building which housed the Officers Club Room on the second story. The chapel was on the ground floor which was also used for a library and reading room, concerts, lectures, court martials,

Father E. W. J. Lindesmith, Chaplain at Fort Keogh, Montana Territory—1880.

school quarters for soldiers and children. Services were held on the holy days and few holidays, Christmas, Memorial and Thanksgiving observances.[6]

Besides his duties as chaplain of the Fort, Father Lindesmith took care of the spiritual needs of the Catholics in Miles Town. His first baptisms were held in the court house on August 22, 1880. Francis and Edward, sons of John Darcy and Sarah Rooney Darcy, received the sacrament.

Mass was offered in the public school house on the same day and announcement was made that on all Sundays after Mass, a sermon and confessions at Fort Keogh, there would be the same program with catechism at 11:30 for the people of Miles.

Father Lindesmith organized a catechism class November 28, 1880, in the public school, a log cabin, 25 by 14 feet. This was the first catechism class in eastern Montana. He called it "The Golden Class." Membership consisted of the children of three families: William and Ann Murphy; Charles, Amora, Abigail and Mary Payette; and Katherine Burke.[7]

Both Father Lindesmith and George Yoakum were instrumental in obtaining the Ursulines from Toledo for the Cheyenne Indian Missions.

Father Lindesmith gives this account of his attempt to obtain Sisters:

In March, 1881, I wrote Bishop (O'Connor) that there ought to be a convent of nuns in Miles City. The secretary wrote me that the Bishop will try to get them from Montreal. May 1, 1881, he wrote me that he could not get the Sisters, but for me to write to Missoula, that perhaps I could get Sisters from there. I never wrote them because I knew they could not spare them.

"Bishop Gilmore of Cleveland had promised me to send a priest and six Sisters for Miles City and for the Cheyenne Indians. But he did not send them until the Bishop applied for them. Then he sent them immediately."[8]

Bishop Brondel appealed to Bishop Gilmore of Cleveland, Ohio, for a group of Sisters to work among the Cheyennes.

Bishop Gilmore then wrote to Bishop Brondel of the offer of the Ursulines of Toledo to go to the Indian Missions. "I will be glad to let a colony go for such a purpose and will give them my Godspeed with all my heart, rejoicing that the diocese is blessed in its offering."[9]

Six Sisters were selected for the Mission: Mother Amadeus Dunne, Superior of the group, Sister Sacred Heart Meilink, Sister St. Ignatius McFarland, Sister Francis Seibert, Sister Angela Abair and Sister Holy Angels Carobin.[10]

Father Lindesmith's zeal extended beyond his duties as an army chaplain. The Catholics in the new town of Miles City had been visited by a priest from Bismarck, North Dakota. No other priest resided in what is now eastern Montana. It was Father Lindesmith who procured property for a church in the new town, and with the help of a few zealous Catholics, erected a small building.

He is described by one of the pioneer Ursulines:

"We like the Rev. Gentleman very much; he is kind, energetic, wholesouled man, independent, original; his very appearance seems to say, 'God and my duty. I care for nothing else' "[11]

The eastern section of Montana was under the jurisdiction of Bishop James O'Connor of Omaha, Nebraska. In 1877, he visited the territory and administered confirmation in several churches, including those in Helena, Virginia City, St. Ignatius Mission, [12] Fort Shaw and Fort Benton. Bishop O'Connor returned to Omaha by steamboat down the Missouri.

It was to this bishop that both Father Lindesmith and George Yoakum wrote asking for Sisters to help christianize the Cheyennes.[13]

Soon a Bishop was named for Montana. Bishop Brondel wrote:

It was His Holiness, Leo XIII, who, on the 26th of September, 1879, appointed us Bishop of Vancouver Island; who, on the 23rd of April, 1883, transferred us to the vicariate of Montana; and who, on the 7th of March, 1884, erected the see of Helena, appointing us its first Bishop.

28

Mother Amadeus Dunne

The recollection of having erected this Diocese in the Rocky Mountains brought great pleasure to the Sovereign Pontiff. In audience had in 1890, His Holiness told us that in 1844, when Nuncio at the Court of Brussels, he had met the illustrious Indian Missionary, the Rev. Father De Smet, S.J., on his return from his first visit to the aborigines of Montana. His Holiness also was eager to know the condition of the present population, and the means employed for the education of the young generation.[14]

Bishop Brondel was a native of Bruges, Belgium, born February 23, 1842. His early education was received in the schools of the Xaverian Brothers of that city. He then attended St. Louis College in Bruges for ten years. After deciding on a missionary career, he went to the American College at Louvain and was ordained a priest on December 17, 1864, for the diocese of Nesqually, under Bishop A. M. Blanchet. Father Brondel's journey to his mission took him through Panama and up the west coast to Vancouver.

For ten years he was stationed at Steilacoom on Puget Sound, then at Walla Walla, returning after a year to Steilacoom. He built churches both at Olympia and Tacoma.

Father Brondel was consecrated Bishop of Vancouver Island on December 14, 1879, succeeding Bishop Seghers who was appointed Archbishop of Portland, and he remained in that territory until named Vicar Apostolic of Montana, April 7, 1883. Up to that date, the eastern part of Montana Territory was administered by the vicar apostolic of Nebraska. On March 7, 1884, the see of Helena was erected, and Bishop Brondel was named its first bishop.[15]

Later, as Archbishop of Portland, Archbishop Seghers, on his return trip from Rome, stopped to visit his old friend in Helena. Continuing on to Portland he made his farewell to the people of the archdiocese and went on to Alaska and martyrdom.[16]

On October 24, 1883, Bishop Gilmore, in a letter to Mother Stanislaus of Toledo, stated:

I have today written Rt. Rev. John B. Brondel, Helena, Montana, of your offer to go to the Indian Missions, and in time will hear what he has to say. I will be glad to let a colony go for such purpose and will give them my God-speed with all my heart, rejoicing that the diocese is blessed in its offspring.

And so plans were made; Bishop Brondel wrote to Father Lindesmith requesting him to obtain board and lodging for the Sisters until they could rent, buy, or build or change lodging. Bishop Brondel wrote to Bishop Gilmore on December 31, 1883:

Your favor of Christmas day reached here this evening and it sounded like the song of the angels and was heard from the East to the West of America, *Gloria Deo et in terra Pax.*

I have written to Fr. Lindesmith the happy news and I told him that I would send him soon some money for that mission. Your arrangements are perfect and I will do my best to cooperate and make it a success here with the grace of God. If anything would be wanting to send them out, please let me know.

And what shall I say to you in thanksgiving for that fine Christmas present? Well, I shall say nine Masses for the success of the missionaries and for the health and blessing of the Bishop who sent them.

The Ursulines left Toledo Tuesday the fifteenth and arrived in Miles City at the Northern Pacific Depot at 11:45 A.M., Friday, January 18, 1884. The first one to greet them was Bishop Brondel "with outstretched arms, his face beaming with joy, his eyes brimful of tears." The next was Father Lindesmith. Many people were at the depot, among them Mrs. Keenan and Mrs. Coleman. Carriages driven by Mr. and Mrs. Coleman waited to take them to Bridget McCanna's boarding house.

First home of the Ursuline at St. Peter's. Taken about 1887.

We drove up in our fine carriages to a whitewashed log cabin with a Chinese laundry attached to it, the two cabins forming one building. Over the Chinese establishment were the words, Yelee Laundry. From our hostess' door projected a white cotton flag on which was lamp-blacked, "Lodging Rooms." The door was ajar so we walked in and poor dear Mrs. McCanna came in with a dry salute, "You're welcome." While we were trying to get seats, the Bishop and Father Lindesmith and Father Eyler, who walked from the depot, came in.

The grandchildren were dispatched to the neighbors for chairs. The room was cold, the one window in the room was nearly falling out of the frame. The Bishop and myself tried very hard to fasten the door but could not succeed as the latch was out of order, so I backed my chair up to the door to keep it closed. Since I did not get pneumonia that day I think I am secure for the future as the Bishop remarked it was the coldest day he had spent in Montana.

Our good Bishop left us; we then had our dinner which consisted of cod-fish and potato, tea and jelly cake. After dinner we were conducted to our sleeping quarters.

No fire in the room, of course. Snow had blown in through door and window. The moonlight was seen through the openings of walls and roof. The partitions between us and the other lodgers (bar-room tenders, ditch diggers, cowboys, ranchmen, etc.) consisted of pink striped calico stretched across the studding. . .we spread out a blanket and couched all together in Oriental style, wrapped up in shawls and blankets and Father Eyler's overcoat. We regaled ourselves with the remnants of the hamper and talked of home to while away the time till morning, and thus we passed our first night at Bridget McCanna's.[17]

The next morning, Saturday, Mother Amadeus set out searching for a suitable house for a convent. Accompanied by a real estate agent, they found a little brown house with five rooms at $25.00 a month rent. It was situated on the corner

33

of 7th and Palmer Streets. They then went shopping for stores and necessary furnishings.

Sunday morning, the Feast of the Most Holy Name, found us in church at a very early hour, cleaning it, making preparations for His Lordship's presence. The Bishop said Mass at eight o'clock; High Mass at eleven o'clock celebrated by Father Eyler — the first High Mass they ever had in Miles City. The Nuns sang Dumont's *Missa Regia* in D Minor, the Bishop and Father Eyler joining in a Mass so familiar to them. It was really beautiful. The people wept for joy — old and young were beside themselves. Sister S. Heart accompanied as confidently as though she had been presiding at the organ for years. Srs. S. Heart and Holy Angels sang at the Offertory, the *Jesu Dulcis Memoria*. . .

When we returned home to get our breakfast it was two o'clock in the afternoon and callers came flocking in, forgetting that we had not yet broken our fast and not knowing of the vigil that we had been obliged to keep Friday and Saturday nights. . . .The Bishop came to see us Sunday afternoon about 4 o'clock and remained until nearly seven, telling us all about his missionary life. . . .

The town is very dull. There are over 2000 inhabitants but everything is at a standstill. The prices of provisions are enormous. I went out Saturday evening to get some little provisions in to keep us alive. Flour is $10.00 per barrel so we bought only a sack; eggs, $1.00 per dozen, that is ranch eggs; stale eggs are 65¢ per dozen. . .three pounds of tea, 5 lbs. of coffee, and engaged a quart of milk per day at 10¢ per quart. Then we went to the butcher shop and bought 16 lbs. of potatoes, 3 lbs. of bologna, and 6 lbs. of meat at 20¢ per pound. So we commence housekeeping in Miles City. . . .[18]

Sister St. Ignatius teaches the "High School," consisting of 8 girls. Sr. Sacred Heart is charged with the Music, both Vocal and Instrumental. Sr. St.

Francis has the "Primary Department" and does wonders with the children (She has 17 pupils). Sr. St. Angela teaches the boys.[19]

Sister St. Ignatius lists the names of her class:

Mrs. B. McCanna's grandchild, Maggie McCanna, a very bright and good young lady loved by every one; Miss Maggie Hogan from Dakota, a talented child, quite a good education; "Abbie" Payette, one of the elite of our City, very kind, always comes with some kindness from her Mother, not very bright, been at the Convent at St. Paul's; Mary Clifford, a good natured child with talent; Fannie Hurley comes in from the Post, about 3 miles; Josie Prenette from Buffalo, N.Y. very talented, one of the best players in Miles City. . .[20]

It was decided before the Sisters left Toledo that two houses would be established — one in Miles City with three Sisters and the other among the Cheyenne Indians.

A list of regulations were drawn up by Bishop Gilmore that would determine the status of the missionaries in relation to both the Convent in Toledo and their Montana foundations.

The Sisters going to the Montana Missions shall be free to return to Toledo in case of failure or dissatisfaction.

The Indian Mission shall be subject to Miles City House till such time as the Bishop of Montana shall change.

The Superior of Toledo shall not be free to recall the Sisters from Montana but the Sisters shall be free to return.[21]

The Sisters were all anxious to see the Indians and wondered who would be the first to see one. Sister Sacred Heart had a glimpse of someone copper-colored "splitting wood in the yard so rushed in exclaiming, 'Oh, I saw the first

Indian!' " The nuns came to the door, and instead of an Indian, there was John Chinaman with his long queue gracefully twisted on the back of his head!

They were in admiration of the first visitors. Wolf that Lies Down called to see them on the Saturday following their arrival. He had with him Mr. Green, a bartender, and Mr. Rolland, the Indian interpreter. Sister St. Ignatius describes Wolf as "tall and slender, six feet one inch; features, just as history describes the race; complexion, a light copper color; his expression, intelligent, kind and somewhat sad; his face, deeply furrowed with lines of pain and care; his teeth, regular and beautifully white; his fine delicate hands with tapering fingers somewhat astonishes you. He was poorly clad, wore a thin calico shirt (that longs for a bath) and pants made from rough woolen material. His feet were covered with moccasins, and a buffalo skin fell from his shoulders to his knees and was fastened around the waist by a kind of girdle. He carried a bow and several arrows ingeniously made." After greeting them, he sat for some time gazing at them in silent admiration.

He called again on Sunday and that time gave each one a regular *"Pax Tecum."*[22] Imagine it, a real *Pax Tecum* given with all the grace, dignity, and respect of a cleric of the sanctuary. How I wish you could have seen this poor Indian as simple and as respectful as a child endeavoring by gestures to make us understand how pleased he was to have us come. . . .Well, he stayed with us this Sunday afternoon about an hour, and after refreshing himself with part of our dinner, shook hands, made a low bow, and departed.

We have not seen him for the last three weeks, wondered why he was not around but learned yesterday from Yellow Horse that he had gone to Pine Ridge, Dakota, after two hundred and seventy-five Cheyennes. Just before he started he came very early one morning, almost frozen, seemed troubled and excited and tired, to tell us he was going, but we could not understand him. Mother took him to the chapel, showed him how to kneel.

White Bull, the great Cheyenne warrior, was a frequent caller. When they took him to the chapel he was attracted by a picture of the Sacred Heart, and repeated to the Sisters what Father Prando had told him, and added, "If God had come to the Cheyennes, they would not have killed him."[23]

On Thursday, February 14, Father Eyler accompanied by Mr. Toner, an Irish Catholic of this place, started for the Indian camps. They intended visiting Two Moons, White Bull, Black Wolf, Brave Wolf, and Wolf-that-Lies-Down who is a petty chief under Two Moons. They intend to remain eight or ten days; the journey to the Rosebud camp takes as long as to go from here to Toledo, that is, three days.[24]

The Bishop originally intended the Mission to be located on the Rosebud in the territory of Two Moons' band. Father Eyler left with Mr. Toner in a sleigh that February 14 to find a suitable site. He decided against the Rosebud location and purchased land from Mr. Sam Cook which had a three-room cabin on it. This was in the land of White Bull and his Indians.

The property had been taken as a homestead by a George Smith who sold it to a Kit Lamb. While the owner went to work to earn money, he permitted Sam Cook to live on it. When Lamb returned, Cook refused to turn it over to him (in other words, he jumped his claim). Sam Cook sold the property to Father Eyler for $600.00.

Father Eyler returned to Miles City with a report of his mission, then started on March 12, to "begin life as a missionary."[25]

Sister Sacred Heart, Sister Ignatius, and Sister Angela were the original ones selected for the Cheyenne Mission. Mother Amadeus accompanied them. "We intended to follow so as to arrive here on the feast of St. Joseph, but the weather became warm, melting the snow and ice, rendering travel in the mountains impossible."[26]

"The government has given us a transportation outfit, an

37

ambulance and army wagons — an escort and a sergeant to direct the route. Our Post Quartermaster Sgt. Forbes, was instrumental in obtaining us this favor, and thus he saves us considerable expense."[27]

Sister Sacred Heart gives a complete account of the journey.

You can well imagine the hurry of packing in our limited quarters; we did the greater part of it in the stable, but on the appointed day, Thursday, March 27, we were ready to receive marching orders at the time appointed, 9:00 A.M. Father Lindesmith came from Fort Keogh at 7:00 to say Mass for us and see us off. He said the detachment were making their preparations and would be over the river in a short time. By 12 o'clock we had received no news and at three a telegram saying, "We cannot ford the river." By Saturday the Military had made their second arrangements and we prepared for a second start.

With sad hearts we parted from Sr. Holy Angels and Sr. Francis, and our little home in Miles; accompanied by Sergeant Beck and Mr. Toner, we hurried through the streets and across the R. R. Bridge to the ambulance.

We had been told that the road over which we were to travel was dangerous but when we saw the flashing eye and courageous countenance of our driver, MacNeal, we felt confident that he would carry us through and were not disappointed. To see some of the steep hills, washouts, etc. we had to cross, one would say it is impossible, but he, reining up his four pet mules, Pink and Blue, Pet and Baby, would carry us ever so gently down some rocky place and just at the right moment with a cheering whistle and crack of the whip we would be spinning up the opposite side.

But pardon the digressions. Saying goodbye to those who had accompanied us from Miles, we mounted the ambulance and after passing Ft. Keogh saw, so to speak, the last vestige of civilization disappear.[28]

The road winds along over the buttes and becomes more and more rugged the farther south we advance. Before starting, Father Lindesmith had given us many privileges. In his own quaint way he said, "Now when you are traveling, you must not think of fasting, saying your Office and the like. The soldiers will cook a little something for you and they have meat three times a day, and you must take it, too, so that you can stand the journey." We had reason to appreciate his permissions before we got "home."

After riding about two hours over the crags and bad lands and having some pretty good tosses and bumps, just as we were emerging from the hills to the valley, a charming sight met our view. About a half a mile on the bank of the river the soldiers were putting up the first camp. I forgot to say our goods had started in advance. The soldiers were all busily engaged, some putting up tents, others building the fire, old Burke cooking coffee, others taking care of the mules, carrying water, etc., etc.

Our tent (Maj. Logan's) was not up yet so we were requested to remain in the ambulance as the ground was damp. We did so and watched the soldiers pitch the tent, put in a Sibley stove, carry wood, start the fire, put up our cot beds, carry our bed clothing (it was wonderful they did not spread them for they would not let us do anything) and then quietly return to their own quarters, leaving us to enjoy the fruits of their labors.

Father Eyler told us that he was obliged to eat meat on Friday when he went to "Rosebud." We pretended to be scandalized at this, so Mr. Toner determined to make us scandalized at ourselves. We had furnished our hamper and intended to have lunch from it when bacon, potatoes and onions were brought to us from the campfire. We could not refuse (and our appetites were sharpened by the ride) for Mr. Toner sat quietly down at the table (one of the cot beds) and insisted in our doing justice to the soldiers' fare. We managed the bacon and the potatoes but when it came to the onions we were obliged to decline. Then, Mother, the coffee; how I wish Toledo could have seen it. Tongue River is as muddy as the Maumee, so imagine a pail of water dipped from it and boiled with the taste of coffee added. We put in condensed milk and tried to settle it, but all we had was mud. For politeness sake we drank or rather swallowed it, but when pressed to have more, declined. After supper we washed the dishes and went over to the campfire to see the boys bake biscuits for the next day. They mixed a large quantity of flour, baking powder and water together, kneaded it into large lumps and threw it into the Dutch oven heating over the fire, then tightly covering the oven and placing it between the coals, in about half an hour showed us quite a fair looking biscuit.

After this, Sergeant Beck posted the guard for the night and we retired to our quarters. One would think that sleeping under canvas would give us all a good cold, but to say the least, no, our tent was so comfortable and warm that even Mother Amadeus did not take the least cold or suffer from rheumatism. We were all very tired, so soon sweet sleep came to refresh and strengthen us. Mr. Toner insisted on keeping the fire up for us during the night. To this, however, we refused to accede, not caring to have anyone see us in our little beds (Do not be scandalized at what I am telling you, Mother), so with a good supply of wood for the night, we fastened our tent door and retired. We did not undress during the entire journey.

The next morning the Reveille and Bugle (a tin pan and a soldier's whistle) awaked us; as we were not as prompt in answering as the soldiers nor as hasty in our toilets (a good shake and wash at the river completed theirs), our breakfast was suddenly handed to us by raising the tent partly from the ground. Bacon, potatoes and mud coffee again. During the night snow had fallen about one inch in depth, so while the soldiers were pulling up the stakes we enjoyed a little walk and quenched our thirst with the beautiful snow. At about eight o'clock we were ready to take up the line of march. The scene reminded me of a picture in one of our old geographies, the canvas-covered wagons with four mules attached, the ambulance, the soldiers, and our shy and quiet sergeant on his pony, called St. Patrick, with the gun swung across his saddle.

In about half an hour we came to a shack where we obtained a drink of water. Oh, what a grateful boon it was to us. In two hours we were well into the buttes again, at one time on the summit, then in the valleys, when the road led quite suddenly around the side of a hill and we were asked to alight and walk as there was danger of the ambulance falling into a gulch on the lower side of the road. We did so, and the men, before they would venture to drive the team across, went to work with pick and shovel to level the road. The ambulance and first wagon with great care and dexterity were gotten safely over. The second wagon, coming a little near the edge, and the ground a loose clay giving way, we saw the wagon gently sliding down the embankment, dragging the mules after it. We were terrified but the soldiers, after a glance at the debris, said, "Now, you are happy" to the mules, and went to work to extricate them. The poor animals were not injured, and after being released, had a good roll on the grass and commenced grazing as though nothing had happened. Fortunately, army transports are very strong and only the tongue of the wagon was broken and, as extra ones were provided, in three hours we were ready to continue our march.

This was Passion Sunday and Mother's Feast, but our situation must be borne. While we were waiting for the wagon to be repaired and loaded, we were taken on a short distance out of the wind, and as it was raining slightly, our good wagon master, Mr. Toner, and Mr. MacNeal, made us remain in the

41

ambulance while they cooked the feast day dinner for us. A fire was started, a kettle hung over it and soon delicious ham was served us; our hamper provided us with bread, butter, and eggs, the latter brought to us by Father Lindesmith with fried cakes and cookies, a present from his soldier boy housekeeper, Dunne. By this time the wagons were in front of us but only for a short time. In crossing the bed of a mountain stream which was filled with quicksand, one of the wagons got mired. Now for more work for our soldier boys. After vainly trying to get the mules to pull it out, and as MacNeal very philosophically remarked, "When a mule won't, he won't," the wagon had to be unloaded and lifted out by the men.

Soldiers are noted for their profanity, but let it be said to their credit, during the whole time no irreverent word was heard. In these vexations, the Sergeant was so quiet and careful that his men were obliged to keep cool also. On we went again; time was beginning to seem long to us, so we entoned the *Ave Sanctissima.* We had not entered upon a plain and were told we were coming to a well populated town; looking out we could not see a human habitation but little mounds of earth covering the surface of the plain. Soon we heard the shrill bark of the prairie dog and then understood all. A few shots were fired at them but ineffectually, and we did not have the pleasure of a closer examination. It was now near the end of our second day but the patience of the men must have one more trial. A piece of gumbo must be crossed; the poor mules were nearly worn out but by attaching an extra pair for the crossing, with beating and shouting the poor animals were urged over and out.

A woody little spot near the river was selected for our second camp, but this night we were to have company. A band of Indians reached the spot at the same time, threw down their packs, unloaded their ponies and the squaws commenced pitching the tents while the braves sat on the hill above, surveying the labor. It was a painful sight to see these great strong men lazily stretch themselves upon the grass while their squaws, some of them with papooses upon their backs and others clinging to their sides, performed all the labor, unloaded the ponies, pitched the tent, chopped and carried wood, built the fire, etc. A strange contrast indeed in this lonely spot in the wilderness between civilization and barbarity, Christianity and heathenism; in one camp the woman, the poor degraded slave; in the other, every honorable and refining care lavished upon her.

A painful incident occurred on this second day which I forgot to mention before. Mr. Toner, in trying to assist in crossing a bed of quicksand, had his hand caught in the harness and as he endeavored to loosen it the snap of the bridle caught a ring on his finger and drew it off. It was his dead wife's wedding ring, he told us after that; her last conscious act was to take the ring from her finger and place it on his. He felt the loss of it most keenly; search for it was useless.

The following day we spent in about the same manner, except that we had to ford a river. After one miring of the team we came to what is called Williams' Ford. The river is narrow, about 50 ft. wide, but had a very swift current; the water, too, was very high. As the ambulance was the lightest it had to cross first; we felt danger but resolved to show no signs of fear, so sat quietly in our places, expecting each moment to be overturned and to get a cold bath, to say the least. MacNeal showed himself equal to the occasion, drove against the current, kept the wagon from floating and in a few moments we were on terra firma again. We then stopped at Williams' ranch and Mrs. W. came out to see us. She was the first white woman we had spoken to since we left Miles and the second we had seen. This day we had no dinner, travel was pretty good and we must make as many miles as possible. One delay in the afternoon, quicksand again, the miring of a wagon, building of a corduroy bridge, a laughable incident which I cannot omit, and our third day's work was done. While waiting for the wagons to be carried across we alighted from the ambulance and took a walk. On our return it was thought best for us to cross the corduroy afoot and the ambulance to be driven over unloaded. The bridge partly gave way under the pressure and the ambulance gave such a bound that MacNeal was thrown from his seat to the ground between the mules. This to him was disgraceful, extremely so; we expected to see him trampled upon every moment. The men shouted at the mules, trying to stop them, and MacNeal with a desperate spring regained his seat and throwing his leg over the upper part of the seat and letting it hang in a lifeless way cried out, "Broken leg, broken leg." This changed the alarm to mirth and soon we were pleasantly rolling on again.

On the morning of the fourth day we forded the river a second time and, passing on some distance, were fastened in the undergrowth, which we attempted to pass through, owing to the roads having been washed away by the late floods. After a little hard work with the axe we were able to get through as the road was higher. We were now on the off hills of the Wolf Mountains. We were told we would reach "home" by noon. This morning we were also joined by the wagons belonging to the citizens, carrying our provisions under the charge of Mr. R. J. Toner, Dick or Old Dick as the people called him although he is only twenty-eight, a quiet gentleman but a confirmed bachelor. About 11:00 o'clock Father Eyler met us. Three weeks as a missionary had worked great changes in him physically. He had grown so thin you would scarcely recognize him. Then he was so brown and sunburned. He seemed glad to see us.

The mail boy. Pray for us. S.S.H.[29]

They reached their new home at 12 noon on April 2. The soldiers worked all afternoon doing everything they could to make the shack livable. Sister Angela Abair writes:

We found an empty log house that had not been used for a long time. The afternoon was a busy one. The men unpacked the wagons, made an altar of rough boards, a kitchen table, and a few stools to sit on. The box which the organ came in was transformed into a cupboard for our china and tin ware. Some of the men mended the old stove that we found in the shack, brought water from the river bank so we could get down without falling. One man was asked to go to Mr. Tim Cook, the nearest white man, who lived about two miles away, to get some hay to fill our bed ticks.

As soon as the nuns could, they covered the ceiling and back of the altar with muslin to hide the fancy sacks that kept the mortar from falling. The altar was fixed; the calico curtains for the sanctuary were made. The No. 8 stove was cleaned and the plank floor mopped. It was nearly morning by this time, and we lay on the floor for a little rest.

The men returned to the Fort the same day, and we were left to manage as best we could. Mother Amadeus left two days later for Miles City in an Indian wagon with White Bull and his little girl, Yellow Stocking. How Mother fared she never would tell. She only said, "God knows."

Sister Ignatius describes their new home in the wilderness, a shack, as they called it, a log cabin of three rooms. The school room was in the middle, the Sisters' apartment to the right, and that of Father Eyler to the left. The floor and roof were of mud, the desks made from the baggage boxes that came from Toledo and Miles City. The blackboard for a while was the mud floor until a gift of one came from Toledo. This was fastened to a door found in the stable and rested on two barrels. A few sacred pictures hung on the walls and attracted the attention of the Indians.

The Sisters had brought three cots with them but they

gave one to the priest, so one nun slept on a table.

Their joy was great.

Need I tell you, Mother, how much I enjoy teaching the darling little children of these vast and lonely wilds. Within that mud-roofed and floorless hut I have experienced more real joy than years gave me beneath our frescoed walls; more than once have our souls been inundated with delight and tears of joy flow unbidden at the sight of our half-clad Cheyennes kneeling before the altar with hands joined and eyes riveted on the Crucifix, the Sacred Heart, or a picture of Our Bl. Lady which rests on the altar. If joy so indescribable as experienced now when we have the means of doing almost nothing, what will it be when God enables us to take those darlings under our own roof to wash, clothe and feed their famished souls — for this are we praying, and for this we beg your prayers, dear Mother, and those of our beloved Sisters.[30]

The schoolroom is the middle division of the shack, Rev. Fr. Eyler's apartment to the left, and ours to the right — log walls with mud cement, readily conducting the sound to either division. The room is about 12 ft. square with a façade of vertical pine logs, unhewn, the remaining walls horizontally laid. It is about eight feet high with mud roof, *mud* floor hardened by occasionally watering it with brine; one window of six panes of glass, common size, we have to make a little stoop to take a view, etc. — the door and window were put in since our arrival by Mr. R. Toner, one of our Miles City friends. My "Normal School Desks" are the baggage boxes from Toledo and Miles, the veneering, ornamentation, etc., quite profuse, as the rough road travelled left a deep impression — the "blackboard," for a time was the mud floor, a very convenient one, neither chalk nor erasure necessary; the present one, thanks to you, dear Mother, is immeasurably better. Having no smooth plastered wall to which to tact it, and a *board* being a rarity here, the dilemma was how we could manage the highly prized manilla, when the thought of a door in the stable came to our relief, and upon this our manilla is tacked, the door rests horizontally upon two barrels answering as supports at either end; the whole supplies, usefully if not beautifully, the present need as a means of illustration. There hung upon our mud-frescoed walls a few sacred pictures which arrest the attention, not only of the children, but also the parents, and help us greatly in giving them some idea of God, of the "dear Mother of God," St. Joseph, etc. Over the little window that faces the West, there hangs a picture of the Sacred Heart, and to this the Indians are particularly attracted — it is a touching sight to see the poor souls gather around it and gaze upon it, making at the same time a low, sad moan, and when we explain it, the faces become sadder and very often tears fall from the eyes. There was one old Indian that particularly affected us; it seemed as though his look at the loving Heart could not be satisfied; he evidently had some knowledge of what the picture represented, and in a little while commenced to pray. We asked him what he said to Am-aur-ho, and he told us he asked Am-aur-ho to send the Cheyennes something to eat. I must say, Mother, the dear old Indian of seventy snows touched my very soul. After telling us he saw "heap a-pow-a" in our eyes, that he could see in the eyes that *we were good*, he bade us goodbye. Pardon me, Mother, I fear I've run away from school; I must return — I left off at the blackboard, no, the pictures. I think I have mentioned every piece of furniture except the teacher's stool, and one of Rev. F. Eyler's boxes that serves as a desk or table. Such, Mother, is our first Indian school, rude enough indeed, and little adapted to elevate our swarthy children, but we feel that God will soon give us the means more likely to attract and improve. Not knowing the language, teaching and learning, will be slow; and yet it is

47

First convent and school – St. Labre's Mission

astonishing to see how much they can understand by gestures. The children are quite apt and love their books and slates. I wish you could see the little darlings write, and here a father, or there a mother, looking intently at a papoose and often helping the child to understand; yes, not only the children come to school, but father and mother and often after wading the river about the knees. Really, Mother, I think the Indian's love for his offspring is marvelous.[31]

After Mother Amadeus returned to Miles City, Chief White Bull came to church with his little Yellow Stocking. Sister Francis wrote:

We had Mass this morning at eleven, as usual, subject of the sermon was "The Upright Woman," during which there was a loud rap at the door; it was opened by one of the trustees; next I heard Father Lindesmith say, "Give them seats. They won't scalp you." It was White Bull and his daughter, Yellow Stocking, and another Indian. They were wrapped in blankets of different colors. This was the first time an Indian was ever seen in church at Miles City. The Chief knelt down, he wore a medal of the Immaculate Conception around his neck fastened to a large brass chain. His daughter came and sat with Mother and me; we sit behind the children. . . . We were escorted home by our Indian friends who were standing in the road waiting for us. We created quite a little sensation in the town; the people appeared to enjoy the show of the Nuns, the Indians and our boarders. White Bull visits us frequently.[32]

This same Indian, White Bull, had taken an active part in the Battle of the Little Big Horn.[33] Father Lindesmith himself baptized him at Fort Keogh.[34]

In a short time Father Joseph Eyler's health began to fail. On June 8, 1884, Sister Sacred Heart wrote to Mother Amadeus, "A new and heavy cross has come to us. Rev. Father Eyler left us this morning. I think I told you in my last letter that his health was very poor; during the past month he has suffered greatly from his lungs, and becoming rapidly worse, he told us on the feast of St. Angela that he intended to leave; we thought he would wait some time at least, go to Miles to consult a doctor and wait until he had received word from the Bishop. Imagine our surprise when he told us last Friday that he was going to Miles and did not intend to return. . . .He was very much grieved over leaving us without a priest, cried bitterly this morning, yet felt that if he delayed longer it would be impossible for him to travel to Miles."[35]

Father Eyler wrote from Miles that "in the name of God I will return to the Basin of O., as the Dr. said."[36]

The situation was discouraging even for courageous souls. Sister Sacred Heart wrote after Father Eyler's departure:

Our poor mission! We thought our trial hard before on account of the Indians and this situation becomes worse as time wears on. The whites seem determined on their removal; Captain Ewers, acting as agent at present, announced that their supply of provisions was exhausted; no more rations until Congress appropriates a fund for their relief; and now no spiritual support for ourselves — O pray for us, Mother, that we may have the courage to persevere. We are all determined not to give up the mission, we are willing to bear anything for the work, and feel confident that God will not reject our united prayers.[37]

Sister Sacred Heart at St. Labre's Mission wrote to Mother Amadeus, Superior, on June 22, 1884:

Mr. George Michael Yoakum is here part of the time, but he is not in favor with the whites, stands in constant fear of some of them, for interference between them and Indians; he is a poor simple-minded man who means well, but who rather injures than promotes the cause of the Indians.

George Yoakum was a member of the 5th Infantry U.S.A. In 1883, his enlistment expired in the Army, but continued (about three years more) working for the Indians for nothing until Congress appointed an agent. The government sent him to the Tongue River country to locate the Indians on the land. Herds of cattle were already grazing there, so trouble was inevitable between the cowboys and Indians. Yoakum was a convert. Father Lindesmith said that Bishop Brondel confirmed him on October 21, 1884.[38]

After Father Eyler's departure the Sisters were left alone without any spiritual help. Bishop Brondel wrote to Mother Amadeus and to the Sisters at St. Labre's that he would take Father Barcelo, S.J., from the Crows and send him to them. Father Barcelo arrived at St. Labre's on July 1, and remained until December.

He experienced a frightening incident which may have affected his health. George Yoakum, the ex-soldier, was frequently with Father at the Mission. Sister Angela writes:

One evening while we were saying our prayers there was a timid knock on the door. The nun in charge went to the door and asked who was there. The man answered, "A friend." There was no answer. Sister said, "If you have any business, please consult the Reverend Father next door." For a few minutes all was quiet. Suddenly we hear George Yoakum call, "Father, Father, help me." Then such banging and scuffling was heard in the schoolroom next to our room. It lasted for about five minutes, but to us it seemed an age. Then all was still. In about half an hour we could stand it no longer, so we took a lamp and went to Father's room. The door was open, but the room was empty. The school room was topsy-turvy. We walked all around the house, along the river bank, calling the priest's name but all was silent as a grave. We came back filled with fear of safety of the priest. After praying for a long time we went to bed but did not undress. About midnight we heard a terrible noise in the school room. Our first impression was that the men had returned and had taken our trunk of winter clothing which was in that room. We feared that they might return for us.

Such suspense I shall never forget. Nothing more happened. With the first dawn I crept out and found the school room locked. I went to the back and looked in the window. There was George Yoakum sleeping on the table which he had pulled up to the door, and the heavy trunk was against the table. I hastened to call the other nuns, and our next thought was whether the priest was in his room. We waited anxiously until Mass time. As usual he was on time, but sad and silent. About nine o'clock George Yoakum was around, stiff and bruised, and gave us an account of the happenings of the previous night. He said that four masked cowboys came to the Father's door and refused to go in, but they demanded that he, Yoakum, come outside as they wished to speak to him. He refused until Father advised him to go. They seized and gagged him, and one threatened to use his revolver on the priest if he interfered. After much struggling they took Yoakum a long distance, tied him to a tree and beat him until he promised to leave the country.[39]

[1] Grinnell, *The Fighting Cheyennes*, pp. 383-384. *Reprinted with permission. Copyright 1955 by the University of Oklahoma Press.*

[2] *Letter of General Nelson A. Miles* to R. L. Upshaw, U.S. Indian Agent, Lame Deer. Fifty-eighth Annual Report of the Commission of Indian Affairs to the Secretary of the Interior. Washington, D.C. 1889.

[3] *Woodstock Letters*, vol. 10, p. 225

[4] Lindesmith, Ms.

[5] *Yellowstone Journal*. Oct. 2, 1877.

[6] Lindesmith, *Diary*. March 9, 1880.

[7] *Ibid.*, August 11, 1880.

[8] *Lindesmith Album,* vol. 7, pp. 19,20

[9] Letter of Bishop Gilmore to Mother Stanislaus, October 24, 1883.

[10] Clotilde Angela McBride, *Ursulines of the West,* pp. 29, 30.

[11] *Letter,* Sister St. Ignatius to Mother Stanislaus, February 12, 1884.

[12] St. Ignatius was located outside his jurisdiction but he was asked to visit there.

[13] Palladino, *Indian and White in the Northwest,* pp. 407-409.

[14] Brondel, *Circular to the Clergy of Our Diocese,* Helena, Montana, Feb. 11, 1903.

[15] John Gilmary Shea, *Defenders of the Faith,* pp. 261, 262. *Progressive Men of Montana,* pp. 80-82.

[16] Sister Mary Mildred, S.S.A., *The Apostle of Alaska, Life of Most Reverend Charles John Seghers.*

[17] *Letter,* Mother Amadeus to Mother Stanislaus, Miles City, Montana, Jan. 18, 1884.

[18] *Ibid.*

[19] *Letter,* Sister St. Ignatius to Mother Stanislaus, April 27, 1884.

[20] *Letter,* Sister Holy Angels to Mother Stanislaus, Feb. 24, 1884.

[21] *Letter,* R. Gilmore to Mother Stanislaus, Cleveland, Ohio, Dec. 19, 1883.

[22] "Peace be to you." A religious salutation sometimes called "The Kiss of Peace."

[23] Letter, Sister St. Ignatius to Mother Stanislaus, Miles City, Feb. 17, 1884.

[24] *Ibid.*

[25] *Letter,* Sister Sacred Heart to Mother Stanislaus, dated Feb. 2, 1884.

[26] *Ibid.* con. Feb. 17.

[27] Letter, Mother Amadeus to Mother Stanislaus, March 29, 1884.

[28] *Letter*, Sister Sacred Heart to Mother Stanislaus, Cheyenne Indian Mission, Brandenburg P.O., Montana, April 27, 1884.

[29] *Ibid.*

[30] *Letter*, Sister St. Ignatius to Mother Stanislaus, April 27, 1884.

[31] *Ibid.*

[32] *Letter*, Sister St. Francis to Mother Stanislaus, April 27, 1884.

[33] Stewart, *Custer's Luck*, p. 486 footnotes.

[34] *Letter*, Mother Amadeus to Father Lindesmith.

[35] *Letter*, Sister Sacred Heart to Mother Amadeus, St. Labre's, June 8, 1884.

[36] *Letter*, Sister Sacred Heart to Mother Amadeus, St. Labre's, June 22, 1884.

[37] *Letter*, Sister Sacred Heart to Mother Amadeus, St. Labre's, July 2, 1884.

[38] Lindesmith Ms., p. 99.

[39] Abair, Sister St. Angela, *A Mustard Seed in Montana.*

CHAPTER 4

History of the Northern Cheyennes Told to
Sister Sacred Heart by George Yoakum, Ex-Soldier[1]

The Northern Cheyennes formerly lived on the Great Sioux Reservation near Black Hills, west of Missouri River. When gold was discovered in the Black Hills, many miners took possession of them, although belonging to the Indians. President Grant failed to remove the miners, which displeased the Indians, and they went on the warpath, saying that the whites had stolen the Black Hills from them. About 3000 Sioux and 100 Northern Cheyennes who had gone on the war path were overtaken on the Little Big Horn River on the Crow Indian Reservation by Custer on the 25th of June, 1876, on which date occurred the battle and massacre of Custer and all his men — not one escaped. The Indians lost 36 men and many wounded.

After the massacre, the Sioux and Northern Cheyennes came east of the Wolf Mountains which are between Rosebud and Tongue Rivers, on the present Northern Cheyenne Reservation and it was said by the old soldiers that the Cheyennes went out hunting and finding no game, came back to the Sioux camp and the latter refusing to give them anything to eat, the Northern Cheyennes became angry at this treatment and surrendered to General Miles. He employed about 70 of these Cheyennes as scouts against the Sioux, and they with their families, numbering about 325, remained at Fort Keogh. The remainder of the Northern Cheyennes were sent to Oklahoma.

After the Cheyennes had surrendered, the Sioux Chief, Lame Deer, pretended he wanted to surrender, too, and asked to have a personal talk with General Miles, although in reality he wanted to kill him as they had killed Custer. When Lame Deer came up for the talk. . .he had a gun under his blanket and shot at General Miles. . . .

White Bull struck the gun aside; the bullet missed Miles

55

but killed the bugler. Then Lame Deer and four minor Sioux chiefs were killed by the friendly Cheyennes and soldiers. After this, General Miles thought a great deal of White Bull, and the latter claimed that Miles promised him the present Reservation.

After Lame Deer's death, Sitting Bull, head chief and 3000 followers escaped immediately from the soldiers and Cheyenne scouts and went with all his Sioux east to the Powder River. Then, following the Powder River, they turned north and by rapid movements escaped to Canada before the soldiers could overtake them. The Canadian government gave them no ration, so they started coming to Montana by small parties for the next three years. Finally they were captured and surrendered together, both at Fort Keogh, Montana, and Fort Buford, North Dakota, where they were kept until 1881 as prisoners of war. Then they were all sent to Standing Rock Agency, North Dakota.

One hundred soldiers, among whom was Mr. Yoakum, and 1700 Sioux, were sent down from Fort Keogh, Montana, to Standing Rock Agency, North Dakota, and Sitting Bull and the remainder of the Sioux were sent from Fort Buford to Standing Rock Agency. In the meantime, the Cheyennes got sick in Oklahoma and became dissatisfied; they broke out and came North, killing many white people on their way, until finally they were overtaken at Fort Robinson, Nebraska, near Pine Ridge Agency, South Dakota. One night soon after they had been confined at Fort Robinson, just as the night guard was calling out, "Ten o'clock and all is well," a daughter of Wild Hog made a great noise as a signal to break out of the guard house, which they did. The soldiers were sent out and about 168 were killed. It was said that one infant was found still alive among the dead. The remainder of the Indians were brought back to the guardhouse where they remained for some time, then they were released and sent to Pine Ridge Agency, South Dakota, and finally were allowed to join the scouts who had remained in Montana.

The scouts and their families at Fort Keogh were told that if they became like white people they would remain in Montana, which they very much desired to do. Mr. William Rowland, a white man who could speak Cheyenne and was married to a Cheyenne, was appointed to locate the Indians who desired to settle on the Rosebud River, Montana, under the Indian Homestead Act of March 3, 1875, and George Yoakum was appointed to locate under said Act the Indians who desired to locate on the Tongue River, Montana. This proved in those Indians' case not to be a good plan, for there were already a great many white settlers on both roads and they did not want the Indians removed; but the Indians, on account of their faithful service to the Government, had made too many friends with the authorities and the petitions of the white settlers to have them removed were both defeated and unheeded.

Things went from bad to worse. There were constant frictions between white settlers and Indians for several years and Mr. Yoakum, a friend of the Indians, advised them to buy out all the white settlers they could. This appeared to be a satisfactory arrangement and they bought out several of the white settlers. Then Agent Clifford recommended the Government to buy out all the white settlers who were within the limits of the Indian settlements. The Government adopted this plan and the Government then sent the Indian Inspector, Major McLaughlin, to buy out all the white settlers, which he did at the cost of $119,000.00. He also bought the railroad lands within the limits of the settlements, making the Tongue River the eastern boundary and the Crow Reservation the western boundary. The northern boundary was forty miles on a straight line to the Northern Pacific Railroad, and the southern boundary was 24 miles south of the northern boundary on a straight line of Northern Pacific Railroad. The Government also made a reservation of the settlements. The said reservation contains 486,000 acres which gave each man, woman, and child 340 acres, for there were at the time about 1500 Indians.

Mr. Yoakum, after his conversion, wanted to make civilized Christians instead of civilized heathens out of the Cheyennes, so he addressed himself to Father Lindesmith, then champlain at Fort Keogh, and told him he would like to have a priest and Sisters among the Indians. Father Lindesmith told him to write to Bishop O'Connor of Omaha, Nebraska — Montana being in that diocese at the time. He wrote to the bishop and was told that a priest and Sisters were difficult to obtain at the time, but Mr. Yoakum would not be turned down. He kept on writing to Bishop O'Connor on the matter and finally the latter wrote that Bishop Brondel had been appointed Bishop of Montana and to write to him. He also said that he would give $1500 toward the Mission.

Mr. Yoakum then wrote to Bishop Brondel and received the same answer — that priests and Sisters were hard to get. Nevertheless, Mr. Yoakum kept on writing. About that time Mr. Yoakum was discharged from the army and had to work for his living. He went broke and went to Miles City, took a job at $2.50 a day and board, driving a team of mules. He wrote again to Bishop Brondel and told him that he wished the bishop could send a priest and Sisters among the Indians.

In four or five days two priests, sent to Miles City, stopped at the house of Pat Schaill, section boss, until they could see Mr. Yoakum. The latter was sent for by Pat's boy who told him that Father Barcelo and Father Prando, S.J., wanted to go among the Indians.

Mr. Yoakum then quit his job, and they went about 60 miles up the Tongue River to Ben Walker's. They gave Ben $2.00 to cross the river in a boat. The two continued the journey on foot up to where the Indians were. Fifteen miles further they stopped at night at an Indian home which had been bought from a white man named Dick Crittenden.

The next morning the two started to baptize children under seven years of age. Father Barcelo baptized the Chief's four-day old child in his mother's arms. Father Barcelo baptized and Father Prando engaged the old Indians in conversation. The Fathers kept on until twelve children were baptized in about three hours' time. They finally came to an old medicine man named Shooting Left-Hand, who became a little quarrelsome (boisterous, he told me, but cannot find the word in dictionary) and said he did not want any more Indians baptized until White Bull came back from Arapahoe Agency, Wyoming, where he was visiting. Mr. Yoakum told the priests what he had said, and they decided not to do anything more at that time. The priests went back to Miles City; Mr. Yoakum remained among the Indians.

58

The next winter Mr. Yoakum met Father Barcelo in Miles City. Taking advantage of a friend in a state of intoxication who wanted to go among the Indians to marry a squaw and tried to induce Mr. Yoakum to do the same, Father Barcelo went to the Indians, 80 miles distant. On the trip from Miles City they stopped at the house of a white settler who tried in vain to persuade Father Barcelo not to go among the Indians, that he could not do anything with them. Father Barcelo referred him to the Revolution, 1789, that the French were not better than the Indians, etc., and they then continued their journey.

When they arrived among the Indians, White Bull had returned from his visit, and the drunken man was perfectly sober. They spent the night at White Bull's house. Father Barcelo told Mr. Yoakum to talk religion to White Bull. The latter said that he had been over to the Arapaho Agency and had seen a man preaching with white man's clothes on, and then he said to Father, "And now you come to us with white woman's clothes on." Then he added, "White man no good because you have one God and two religions; Cheyenne believe in one God and one religion."

Mr. Yoakum told the priest what White Bull had said.

The priest replied, "He has good ideas."

The white man then took Father to Miles City free of charge and spoke no more about getting an Indian wife. Father Barcelo said that the driver was a fine man; he even wrote to thank him for his generosity.

On the twenty-third of the following February, 1884, Mr. Toner of Miles City brought Father Eyler in a one-horse buggy to Tongue River, 80 miles distant, and bought Sam Cook's place for $600. Then in March the Sisters came up and started the Mission at the same place. They immediately got fourteen scholars. They had an organ, and after the first Mass Yellow Horse said, "*Mut sotz,*" meaning "grand, wonderful, great."

Soon after, Colonel Barr, Indian Inspector, was sent from Washington and pronounced it grand, too. He said, "The Sisters are doing a great work."

About the time the Mission started, White Bull's brother had a very bad cough and he thought that if he could get some deer meat it would help him, so he went out hunting, leaving his daughter with the chief, White Bull. He remained out hunting until Father Barcelo came. In the meantime his daughter was taken sick. The Indian medicine man gave her up and got the Sisters to see what they could do. She was baptized and anointed. After this, being perfectly conscious, she turned around, gave the priest a holy look and died twenty minutes later.

Sometime after the Mission started, Cowboy Morris shot Iron Shirt, breaking his arm near the shoulder. Father Eyler desired to see Iron Shirt, so Mr. Yoakum went to Jim Sharp's sheep range to get a team. On the way to Iron Shirt it got dark, but there was a full moon. Wandering through the hills until very late, Father Eyler said he had to have some water or else he could not say Mass the next day. Finally they got out of the hills and went to the river, which was very high at the time. They arrived there at five minutes to midnight. They stopped at the house of Iron Shirt that night, and in the morning, which was a beautiful day in June, he made an altar at the end of the wagon and said Mass in the open air. After Mass they went to see Iron Shirt who was very low, his arm being swollen to great size. He was lying down and unable to rise. The priest, through his interpreter, said that he would be well in ten days. He also said he would apply the relics of the saints to the wound and that if the sick man had faith enough to believe, he would baptize and anoint him. Having received this assurance, Father Eyler baptized and anointed Iron Shirt, who then turned his head toward the priest and gave him a holy look. In five days Iron Shirt passed the Mission, making the 200-mile trip to Miles City and back home. It was a great miracle. . . .On his trip from Iron Shirt, Father Eyler baptized six Indian children. Father Eyler left the Mission soon after that and Father Barcelo was appointed in his place.

In the fall of 1881, the Texas Cattle Company brought in 5000 head of cattle, and they made their headquarters at the present Mission site. The winter of 1881 and 1882 being very severe and the cattle not being acclimated, the company lost all their cattle except 146 head. This loss completely broke up the company and George Smith, a married man, held the present Mission site to try to get something out of it for

60

himself and his family. He finally sold out to Kit Lamb. Kit, being a working man, went away to work for several months to get some money to improve his place but he was foolish enough to let Sam Cook, a married man, take his house to live in while he was away. When Kit came back he politely asked Mr. Cook to leave. Cook refused, saying, "This is my place," at the same time giving him a slap, and drove him off. Cook, being the stronger of the two and having the law on his side (because the law gave the possessor the unsurveyed land) held the place on the Mission site until he sold out to Father Eyler for $600.

Soon after, the Mission started. A good-hearted government surveyor ran our line from the north to the Mission. Mr. Yoakum, being at the Mission at the time, told him that he would lay down the Mission nicely for them. Mr. Yoakum, with those around, saw him laying the four corners. After surveying, a homestead right could be filed. The resident priest at the time would not file on the land, but Mother Ignatius, under her worldly name of Bridget McFarland, proved up on 160 acres and immediately gave it to the Mission, and this the Mission still holds.

About the time the Texas Cattle Company located on the Tongue River, across the river and near the mouth of Otter Creek two white settlers took a claim adjoining one another across the river from the Mission. Their names were Rattlesnake Johnson and Hank Adams. It appears that Johnson was jealous of Adams. Some white men happened to come along visiting. They knocked at Adams' door and receiving no answer, they broke the door and found Adams dead—he had been poisoned. They investigated further and found that Johnson had Adams' team. They then blamed Johnson for having poisoned Adams, but were not sure, and they gave the former a chance to escape, which circumstances confirmed their suspicion. They then wanted to get a crowd and lynch Johnson but he had left the country. When Johnson passed through Miles City, he sold his place to a man from Washington, Iowa, who intended to put a cattle ranch on Johnson's place.

Mr. Yoakum heard of this and being interested in the Mission, he determined to purchase it with his own money from the Iowa man to prevent another cattle ranch being so near to the Mission. He made a flying trip to Miles City, saw the Iowa man before he had time to get to Tongue River for he was afraid that if the latter saw the place he would not sell it. Mr. Yoakum immediately entered into negotiations to buy the place, and soon struck a bargain. The Iowa man was saying he did not know what it was; he had not seen the place. Mr. Yoakum, being a shrewd man, bought it for $250, including a house full of stuff for which the Iowa man had paid $200. Mr. Yoakum had no money at the time but had money on deposit with the Government. Mr. Yoakum, being a soldier at the time, went to Fort Keogh, Montana, to get his deposit book and turned it over to the Iowa man for security. This he kept until Mr. Yoakum's time was up in the Army, and then he came and collected the money. This incident, together with the Texas Cattle Company, left a large track of country on Tongue River and Otter Creek practically open to settlement, and when Mr. Yoakum was appointed by Captain Ewer to locate the Cheyenne on Tongue River, he, being a far-seeing man, took advantage of the situation and immediately conferred with White Bull, the chief, who was almost as far-seeing as himself. When Mr. Yoakum told the chief his plan, they both immediately set to work as rapidly as possible to settle up this land before any more white men would come there because it was a very desirable location and the whites wanted to settle there. They both did all in their power to get Indians to take the land as quickly as possible, explaining the situation to them. Mr. Yoakum told the Indians what to do to hold the claims, and he frequently told them that if the white men did anything to them, not to take revenge but to leave it entirely to the authorities. Mr. Yoakum made it a point from the beginning never to lie to the Indians who, having found that out, always trusted him, believed and did everything he told them, so that he had complete control of the Tongue River and Otter Creek Indians.

The white men also found that out, and on that account they became enemies of Mr. Yoakum, because they thought he was too friendly with the Indians. But they could not do anything against him because he was a soldier and Government employee, and the officers at Fort Keogh and those in Washington stood by him.

During this time there was a postmaster named Charles Jennison who kept the postoffice one mile above the Mission, and who started a trading store with the Indians. He got rather greedy and gave them about a handful of sugar for a deer hide, which they could sell at Miles City for $1.50. So, the Indians naturally kicked, and told Mr. Yoakum that they wanted Jennison to do better by them. Mr. Yoakum waited a while for developments, and so many complaints came in about Jennison that Mr. Yoakum decided something had to be done. He took White Bull with him and went to see Jennison about the matter. Mr. Yoakum asked Jennison if he could not do better for the Indians. The answer was, "If they do not want to trade here, they know what they can do."

White Bull took it to mean that they could go to Miles City, 80 miles distant. He said that the Indian ponies would be tired from hunting, that they could not go so far.

Mr. Yoakum asked Jennison a second time if he could not do better by the Indians, and Jennison gave the same answer. Mr. Yoakum and White Bull then went away and saw Mr. Smith who was still living on the present Mission site; and Mr. Yoakum told him that if he would go to Miles City and bring up a load of goods, he could get all the Indians' trade.

Mr. Smith reflected a moment, then said, "I'll do it." He went down and fetched up a large amount of goods.

Mrs. Smith, who could not speak a word of Cheyenne, (nor could the Indian speak a word of English), showed the Indians by signs that she had goods to sell. Then many Indians came to Mr. Yoakum loaded with hides on their backs to go to Smith's to trade, and Mr. Yoakum who could speak fair Cheyenne wrote down in English what the Indians wanted to buy. Mrs. Smith gave them about four times as much for their hides as Jennison had been giving. The Indians were so well pleased that they all went to Smith, and Jennison lost all his trade.

However, Jennison was not angry because he knew that Mr. Yoakum and White Bull had done all they could to make him do better by the Indians.

Jennison had three white men employees, a cook and

others. This being at the beginning of winter, they were afraid of losing their jobs; so two of them — one a big ex-cowboy, the other, a Mexican — determined to take revenge on Mr. Yoakum.

About that time, a Cheyenne chief named "Little Chief," from Pine Ridge Agency, South Dakota, with about fifty of his people came over and wanted the Cheyennes to go over to Pine Ridge to settle. But White Bull who wanted the Little Chief's band to locate on Tongue River argued the point with the latter. White Bull would not allow the Indians to go to Pine Ridge.

While this argument was going on, Mr. Yoakum whose duty it was to look after matters for the Government, went to Little Chief's camp, located three miles up on Otter Creek, to see how many Indians there were and who they were. The Indians showed Mr. Yoakum where White Bull and Little Chief were arguing; but he stayed only a few moments after finding out what he wanted, and then he started over to his house.

White Bull, having a pony there, kindly asked Mr. Yoakum to take it back, because he wanted to stay arguing with Little Chief. Mr. Yoakum gladly accepted the offer because he was on foot. When he got half way back home, he met the ex-cowboy and Mexican, both heavily armed but on foot.

There was something providential about this, as there were so many providential things happening all the time; because at all other times they were on horseback and Mr. Yoakum was on foot. But this time it was the contrary. Mr. Yoakum although a soldier in uniform, did not have his gun with him.

The ex-cowboy said to Mr. Yoakum, "You son of a —, why did you tell the Indians I was cheating them?"

Mr. Yoakum answered, "I did not tell them you were cheating them." He then began to explain how the case was.

The cowboy made a grab for the pony's bridle but Mr. Yoakum being a good horseman, so promptly whirled the pony around that the cowboy missed it by a hand's breadth.

Starting back toward Little Chief's camp on a dead run, Mr. Yoakum kept zigzagging the pony to prevent any shot hitting him or the rider. When Mr. Yoakum got out of pistol range, he looked back, still running the pony, and saw the ex-cowboy trying to get aim at him with a very large pistol, and he continued to do so until they came to Little Chief's camp and saw White Bull. Mr. Yoakum asked White Bull to tell some of the Indians to give him a gun. His request was complied with. Mr. Yoakum examined the gun and told White Bull it was no good. Then the latter told him to go to Wolfear's camp about one mile away, that he had a good soldier's gun. Mr. Yoakum already knew this, so being about 50 yards from Otter Creek, he had to run the gauntlet between the cowboy, the Mexican and the creek. The cowboy and the Mexican ran all the time to overtake Mr. Yoakum who succeeded on arriving at Wolfear's camp.

White Bull, on seeing what was up, suspended the argument with Little Chief, and followed in the chase. He persuaded the Mexican who understood Cheyenne to give up the chase, and then started after the cowboy until both reached Wolfear's camp.

Mr. Yoakum, in the meantime had dismounted, but was not idle. Wolfear willingly gave him his gun with all the ammunition he asked for. Mr. Yoakum put on a cartridge belt containing 20 cartridges, slipped on the Springfield rifle; and standing at attention with finger on the trigger and muzzle of the gun, on his toes, waited for the cowboy to come up.

The latter knowing that it would not do to have the pistol in his hand, put it in his belt as he came up. About two yards from the door, he stopped and watched his chance to get the drop on Mr. Yoakum. The two men stood there about four minutes, having their eyes on each other, Mr. Yoakum with his finger on the trigger all the time.

After a while the cowboy gave up (trying to get the drop on Mr. Yoakum) and opened his pistol belt in front, but was careful not to attempt to draw his pistol. Then he threw down the belt and the pistol as far as he could, and wanted to have a fist fight.

This was too undignified for Mr. Yoakum who continued to stand there like a statue. By that time the place was alive with Indians who had surrounded the cowboy and Mr. Yoakum.

White Bull and Fire Crow stood in the center of a large

circle of Indians which surrounded the two. . . .White Bull made a mark with his finger on the ground and motioned the ex-cowboy not to come across that mark. At the same time speaking in Cheyenne, he said that General Miles had told him if any white man wanted to kill the soldiers, not to let him get away.

The ex-cowboy could not understand White Bull, but Mr. Yoakum did. Finally the cowboy made a dash for Yoakum who still stood in the same position. . . .White Bull grabbed his left shoulder, and Fire Crow, the right one, and held him back. The cowboy looked in one chief's face, then, in the other's, and seeing there was no use for him to get nearer Mr. Yoakum, he turned and walked off to Jennison's place.

Jennison, instead of discharging him, still kept him on, but discharged the Mexican who went to live among the Indians.

Two months later Mr. Jennison sent the cowboy down to Miles City with $175 cash and all the hides he had bought from the Indians. On his trip down Mr. Yoakum met the cowboy to whom he nodded, "How do you do?" The cowboy nodded with a smile. There was an Indian camp near and he did not attempt to settle Mr. Yoakum at that time.

Two or three days afterward Mr. Yoakum met Jennison in Miles City where he learned from him that the cowboy had taken the $175 cash, and sold all the hides, and had left the country; while the Mexican who had stolen $35 from a white man had gotten two years in prison at Deer Lodge, Montana.

[1] Sister Sacred Heart, *History of the Northern Cheyennes,* Ms., Ursuline Archives.

CHAPTER 5

"Seven Years of Famine"

On July 9, 1884, Bishop Brondel wrote to Mother Amadeus the following:

> The Jesuit Fathers of St. Peter's Mission are anxious to have Sisters. St. Peter's Mission is one day's journey from Helena by stage. See here what Father Cataldo, Superior of the Fathers in the Rocky Mountains, writes to me:
>
> In my recent visit to St. Peter's mission the Fathers have agreed to the following arrangement for the Sisters' school at that place.
>
> 1st. We bought a farm adjoining to the mission for $450.00. This we would give to the sisters, who could get the title from the government by having it surveyed and residing there.
>
> 2nd. We would also give two wagon horses, about a $100.00 worth and two milk-cows about $120.00 worth.
>
> 3rd. We would also give $200.00 worth of provisions, as meat, flour etc.
>
> 4th. We would spend about $200.00 in repairing our old house which we would rent to the Sisters for five dollars a year, and in which they could accommodate 20 girls or more; and this for one, two or three years until they would build a house of their own on their own property.
>
> 5th. If, instead of three Sisters, there could be four, one of the Sisters could teach the little boys and get $200.00 a year from the Fathers.
>
> This last agreement should last for one or two years, but no longer than three.
>
> This is all we can do, but there is hope of having

an appropriation from the government, so much per child.

J. M. Cataldo, S.J.

Now there should be some more missionary element; there is room ready. St. Peter's Mission was established for the Indians of the North Eastern Montana, Blackfeet, Piegan, and their descendants, some halfbreeds. There are also now some farms of white people in the country.

Wishing you every blessing, I remain

Your devoted Bishop,
† John B. Brondel
Bishop of Helena

As for the religious advantages, St. Peter's Mission has two residing Fathers who live with a number of brothers in a stone house.

It was agreed that the Ursulines would go to St. Peter's if more help could be obtained from Cleveland or Toledo. On October 9, Mother Joseph from Cleveland arrived in Miles City with a prospective postulant, Theresa Henry, who was received as Sister Santa Clara.

Mother Amadeus then left Miles City with the two novices, Sister Martha Gahan and Sister Mary Golden, and the postulant, Sister Santa Clara, to open a novitiate and school at St. Peter's. The Northern Pacific railroad took them to Helena, where they were guests of the Sisters of Charity of Leavenworth. Bishop Brondel had written to Mother Amadeus telling her that he had a suitable candidate there — Miss Yunk who later became Sister Ursula.[1]

Helena was the nearest railroad point, so the rest of the trip to the Mission was made by stagecoach to the Dearborn, and from there, Mr. Phil Mannix of Augusta drove the group to St. Peter's.

We can well imagine the joy and delight that the first view of the Mission Valley must have given the soul of Mother Amadeus. As the wagon pulled up from the Sullivan Valley, the travelers looked back at a magnificent panorama of the Dearborn River and the Rockies beyond. Turning from this view, the road winds into Mission Valley which opens up into a vision at once startling and inspiring.

A visitor, seeing this for the first time, remarked, "This is a spot I'll always want to return to."

The missionaries were greeted by Father Damiani, S.J., superior, and the Brothers who were always dear to Mother Amadeus. The nuns were happy to take possession of their small log cabins lined up and joined one to the other with a porch down their entire length. Joined by a bell tower by the church, they formed an ell. The missionaries saw the surrounding hills giving them shelter and enclosure. On one side of the road to the north were Fish Back, next a large mountain which they later named St. Ursula, and another topped by a rocky formation, this called Magdalen Rocks. Behind the cabins were Skull Butte, Black Butte with a cave in the side, later christened Martha Cave, Saddle Back, Damiani and Imoda.

The day was October 30, 1884. The Jesuits needed teachers also for the boys' school. Just a year before in June, Louis Riel who taught at St. Peter's had left. He was even now on his way to head another uprising in Canada that finally led to his death on the scaffold.

A group of Métis had come to the Mission and had persuaded him to leave with his wife, Marguerite, and their little daughter. Father Eberschweiler, S.J. who was then stationed among the Gros Ventres, met him and tried to dissuade him from going.

Louis Riel had come to St. Peter's to teach in the boys' school in the summer of 1883. He remained there with his wife, Marguerite, until June, 1884. In September, 1883, the daughter, Marie Angelique, was born.[2]

The annalist recorded in 1891 "Seven Years in Montana — Seven Years of Famine." The little group had entered into their missionary activities with such enthusiasm that they scarcely felt the hardship, isolation, and lack of necessities those first years brought.

The original cabins, built in 1865, were about a quarter of a mile nearer the canyon. The church was begun in 1875 and finished the following spring. It was soon too small for the congregation, settlers and halfbreeds, so an addition was built.

Left—Martha Brown; Center—Teresa Brown; Right—Anna Brown.
Daughters of Mr. & Mrs. John D. Brown.

The settlers around the Mission wished to send their daughters to school. Shortly after the Sisters arrived, Mother Amadeus opened a boarding school for these children on November 10, 1884. The first pupils were Martha and Anna Brown, daughters of John D. Brown, and Mary, or Mollie, Lewis, eldest daughter of Ed Lewis. Soon after school opened, Mother Amadeus with Sister Martha Gahan took the stage for Fort Assiniboine in search of pupils and financial help. Fort Assiniboine was established as a military fort in May, 1879, on the Missouri, forty miles from Coal Banks. Under the command of Colonel T. H. Ruger, the 18th Infantry garrisoned the post. The military reservation extended 40 miles in one direction and 15 in another. Troops were transported up the Missouri by boat as far as Coal Banks, then had to travel overland 40 miles to the Fort.

The Indian school for girls opened on March 7, 1885, with eleven pupils. The children were all of the Blackfoot tribe. They were: Kaminiki, Rose Couquette, Mary Grant, Josephine Couquette, Elizabeth Couquette, Josephine Langlois, Mona Tokomiski and Susie Russell. Only eight names were listed in the original group, but later we find the name of Elizabeth Couquette with entrance date, March 7, 1885. In the original group, only two could read and write.

School was held from 10:00 A.M. to 12:30 and from 2:00 P.M. to 4:00 P.M. Manual work occupied the children from 8:00 A.M. to 9:00, 1:00 P.M. to 2:00 and 5:00 to 6:00. The teachers were Sister Mary Amadeus, Superintendent; Sister St. Gertrude, teacher; Sister St. Martha, industrial teacher.

For texts in reading they used: *Object Word Method*, Baade's *Permutation Case*, McGuffey's *Primary Charts*, Catholic National Series and Primer, First and Second Readers. In penmanship: Slate Exercises, and Payson, Dunton and Scribner's. In arithmetic: Davies *Primary*, *Oral Instruction*. The children were introduced to kitchen work, mending wardrobe, and knitting. Gradually they learned sweeping, butter-making, plain sewing, and later, bread-making and dining room work. This was the beginning. As time went on, they advanced and were taught embroidery, music and art, in which many were especially gifted.

As the enrollment grew, new buildings were added. In

Left—Maggie Lewis; Center—Mollie Lewis; Right—Teresa Lewis.
Daughters of Mr. & Mrs. Edward Lewis.

72

November, 1885, Loretto House was built; in September, 1886, a storehouse. In the *Sun River Press* of March 25, 1886, published at Sun River, we find the announcement that "Tom Moran, Ed Lewis, Rock Gobert, and John Tabor have donated a fine school house for the Sisters and finished it in good shape."

Martha House was constructed during the fall of 1886. The following year in April, a log Indian school was erected and in May, St. Francis Xavier House, all for the use of the children. These were log cabins built in the usual manner of the original buildings. A site was chosen for a new stone building across the road, large enough to care for the needs of the growing schools.

July 7, 1887, was an eventful day at the Mission. Father Bandini drove the first stake, and Mother Amadeus the last, that was to mark the foundation of the new convent.

The laying of the cornerstone was an event, all important in the Mission. The following account was placed in the stone:

> On the ninth day of September, one thousand eight-hundred and eighty-eight, Feast of the Most Holy Name of Mary and the first feast of St. Peter Claver, S.J., the cornerstone (which contains this document) was solemnly blessed and laid with great ceremony by the blessed hands of Reverend Father Joseph Vincent Francis Damiani, S.J., the present Superior of St. Peter's Mission, Montana Territory. During the pontificate of our Holy Father, Leo XIII, when Grover Cleveland was President of the United States of America and Rt. Rev. John Baptist Brondel, Bishop of Helena. Kemp Leslie was governor of the Territory of Montana, Joseph K. Toole was delegate from Montana. Father Damiani, S.J., Sup., Father Mayer, S.J., of St. Louis, Father Herman Schuler, S.J., Brother Claessens (who came to Montana October, 1841, with Father De Smet), Brother Francis and Brother John Negro, Brother Jerome Galdos at this time compose the Jesuit Household. Sister Mary of the Angels from Toledo, Ohio (Professed); Sister

Clementina Pillcod (Professed); Sister Perpetual Egan (Professed); Sister Eugenia Sullivan (Novice); these three from St. Louis, Missouri; Sisters St. Martha (Professed); Helena (Novice) and Marguerite (Novice); Caecilia (Novice); Agnes (Novice); and Sister Rose Marie Galvin (Postulant), and Sister Mary Amadeus (Professed), Superior of the Ursulines of Montana — *these eleven* compose the Ursuline household of St. Peter's Mission, in all, five professed, five novices and one postulant. The Architect and builder of the house is Nicholas Monshausen. May the Peace of Christ dwell in this house of education. May it be erected for the greater honor and glory of God, Mary, and Joseph, St. Angela, Ursula, Augustine, and Charles Borromeo.

Unto Our Lord, to His Sacred Heart are committed all that will ever dwell therein. Jesus, Mary, Joseph.

At the time of the laying of the cornerstone the Ursulines had five Missions in Montana. St. Peter's for the Blackfeet; St. Paul's for Gros Ventres and Assiniboine; St. Labre's for Cheyenne, and St. Xavier's for the Crows. Jesus, Mary, Joseph protect us and bless us.

Father Lindesmith's visit to St. Peter's in 1887 brought much joy to all at the Mission. He knew many of the nuns and had a great interest in all their work in Montana since he, himself, had been instrumental in bringing them to the territory. Mother Amadeus herself once referred to him as the Archfounder.[3]

He left Fort Keogh on July 28 that year for St. Ignatius Mission and from there traveled to St. Peter's. At Helena on August 10, he took the stage which left at 7:20 for the Dearborn and arrived at 9:30 A.M. in Silver City, which he describes as an abandoned mining camp with about fifteen houses and six families. He passed through Prickly Pear Canyon on the way to Dearborn Station. Here he hired a horse and rode to the Mission. The nuns were in retreat. On Sunday, August 14, Father preached to the people who filled the church.

74

He wrote:

One of the Nuns presided at the organ and she did well, the Choir and children sang beautifully, and to my mind, extra sweet, they sang and said prayers in three different languages, viz., Latin, English and Piegan. On the evening of the same day at 6 o'clock the retreat of the Nuns was concluded. On Monday, Aug. 15, after first Mass which I said, I took breakfast with all the Nuns. The breakfast was sumptious, indeed, it had been prepared for my special benefit by Mary Fields, a colored woman who used to live with the Nuns in Toledo, Ohio. She was born in Tennessee, raised in Mississippi. She was a slave until the Emancipation. She came north to Toledo, became a Catholic, and remained with the Nuns ever since. She now runs a hennery of about 400 hens and ducks and a splendid kitchen garden with vegetables enough for the Nuns and Indian girls. She does all the work except the plowing.

Father Lindesmith was amused at Mary's description of her attack on a pole cat which had invaded her chicken coup and killed 62 hens.

The community at this time included Mother Amadeus, Sister Francis, Sister Mary of the Angels, Sister Thomas, Sister Mary, Sister Martha, Sister Helena, Sister Marguerite, and Miss Wiegand, a postulant. Brother Claessens who had come to Montana with Father De Smet in 1841, was at this time living at the Mission and entertained all with his stories of early missionary life and hardships. There were 89 Indian boys and girls in residence at the Mission at this time.

At 4:00 P.M. on August 15, a wagon took Father Lindesmith to the Dearborn where he put up at the Stone Hotel which was kept, as he said, by a Catholic man from Montreal.[4]

Father Eberschweiler asked for Sisters to open a school for the Gros Ventres Indians at St. Paul's Mission at this time. Father Frederick Eberschweiler was born in the Rhine Province of Germany at Wascweiler in 1841. He and his brother entered the Jesuit novitiate in Westphalia and Father was ordained a priest at Maria-Laach. After serving in the army as chaplain he came to the United States and spent some time in Buffalo, New York. Father Eberschweiler was professor at St. Mary's Seminary in Cleveland from 1871 to 1873. He was then sent to Toledo where he was assistant at St. Mary's Church from 1873 to 1881. Back to Cleveland, he was stationed at St. Mary's Cathedral, 1881 to 1882.[5] In August, 1883, he came to the Rocky Mountain Missions and was assigned to Fort Benton with all the surrounding territory as his mission. Father went to Fort Belknap as a missionary to the Gros Ventres and Assiniboine Indians on December 2, 1885. Two years later, 1887, he left the Fort to stay at the Mission he had founded for these Indians in the Little Rockies.

Sister Francis relates that Mother Amadeus had been thinking for some time about the Sisters she would choose. "One day on the way to Vespers, Mother said, 'I have decided who is to go to St. Paul's' 'I am so glad, Mother,' I said, 'You are relieved of that worry.' '*You* are going, Sister, and Sister Martha.' Mother began Vespers; I broke down, couldn't say them. When we were going, Mother felt very badly. I was in the chapel. Mother came in and laid a large crucifix on my lap, kissed me and said, 'Goodbye, Sister,' and left."

The pair left in a lumber wagon for Brown's place where they stayed overnight. The stage route ran past this ranch on Shaw Butte. Next morning they took the stage for Fort Benton. In Great Falls, a stop was made in front of the Park Hotel where the driver had to silence some men whose language he feared would annoy the Sisters.

They spent the night at Fort Benton, boarding the stage for Fort Assiniboine the next day. There they were given hospitality by the Commander of the Fort. The little daughter of this couple had been killed recently by a fall from a horse. The mother thought the Indians had frightened it. How could she understand these Sisters — one, a wisp of a person — going into outlaw territory to teach these Indians?

Next morning the Major came to the Sisters and announced, "The chariot is at the door." They rode as far as O'Hanlon's for another night's stop. The following day several wagonloads of Indians came to welcome them and to see the great engine that was due to arrive soon. The party finally arrived at St. Paul's on September 14.[6]

Two more schools were opened in 1890, one at St. Ignatius Mission and one at Holy Family. The school at St. Ignatius was a kindergarten for the Flathead children. The building at Holy Family was erected by the charity of Mother Katharine Drexel and called the Drexel House. It was located on the Two Medicine River and intended for the Blackfoot Indians.

In March, 1890, Mothers Perpetua Egan, Santa Clara Henry, Martha Gahan and Margaret Mary Langevin opened the new experiment, a kindergarten for the Indian children at St. Ignatius.

Mother Angela Lincoln, Sister Irene Arvin and a postulant, Sister Monica Martin, went in August to Holy Family to begin the school there for the Indians of the Blackfoot tribe, mainly the Piegan.[7]

Father Peter Prando was at the Mission during the Rogation Days in 1891 and led the processions, blessing the fields and praying for a good harvest. In May, Father Cataldo with Father Andreis and Brother Schloir arrived. Father Neil from Baltimore stopped to visit on his way to Alaska. Father Prando then left for the Crow Mission, and Father Damiani for Holy Family.

The Corpus Christi Procession at St. Peter's was an event in which all took part. The girls and women, followed by the boys and men, then the nuns and choir, left the church with twelve little Indian girls in pink dresses and white veils, strewing flowers before the Blessed Sacrament. The procession marched to the Fathers' house, and then back to the church.

This took place on May 31, 1891, the day Father Cataldo chose to inaugurate the Sodality of the Blessed Virgin Mary. Forty-four children were received, eleven from each of the four schools: the girls' academy, the girls' Indian school, and the schools of the Jesuits — white and Indian — for the boys.

Mary Josephine Agessa was born near Chinook, Montana, on the site of the old Belknap Agency. Her father, Bushy Head, was one of the five under-chiefs of the Gros Ventres tribe located on this reservation. When, in 1887, Mother Amadeus asked Father Eberschweiler to bring her six girls from the Gros Ventres country, Agessa was among the favored ones. A perfect type of Indian, she had a high forehead, long aquiline nose, a profusion of straight black hair, and lovely white teeth. She was baptized by Father Damiani, and given the name of Mary Josephine Agessa. She sang well, wrote admirably, drew, painted and carved creditably, and her darning was a marvel.

Agessa fell very ill with pneumonia from which she seemingly recovered, but soon became consumptive. Dr. Adams and Dr. Gordon of Great Falls tried unsuccessfully to save her. Bushy Head and his wife came to see their daughter before she died.

Father Munroe, who was a frequent visitor from Fort Benton, came again to the Mission in June. This dear Father was later a great missionary in Alaska, where he built the first church in Fairbanks. Francis Munroe was born near Lyons, France, in 1855. He was a classmate of Marshal Foch at the College of Metz in Lorraine. At La Providence College in Amiens, in 1873, he had been a fellow student of Francis Crimont, later Bishop of Alaska. The two were also together in the Jesuit Novitiate at St. Acneul, and came together to America in 1886, accompanied by Father Muset, S.J. Archbishop Seghers, who had just been reappointed to Victoria, British Columbia, had often lectured in Father Munroe's classes at Liège. Father Munroe, a missionary stationed at Fort Benton, spent four years at St. Peter's, some time among the Crow Indians, then went on to Alaska.

Father Feusi also came that June. He was working with the Gros Ventres and Assiniboines.

Every year Bishop Brondel attended the closing exercises at the school, administered Confirmation, and presided at the reception of novices and profession of vows. He frequently celebrated his name day (Feast of St. John the Baptist) with the Fathers, nuns and children.

This June 27 he was accompanied by Rev. Muehlsiepen, Vicar General of the Diocese of St. Louis, Missouri. The Mission gave him a colorful welcome. The Indian boys rode out to meet the distinguished guests with flags flying from their horses' heads. Then the Community extended their greetings. They loved their Bishop. On the following day Bishop Brondel confirmed 90 persons, including 11 white girls and 23 Indian girls. Later he visited with the nuns, and the annalist recorded:

He could never express in words his love and appreciation for our Order, his wonder at what God had wrought by our feeble instrumentality. He said we were his first born, that no one could pluck this honor from us. He told us yesterday his love for St. Peter's, his amazement at its growth and development, how it soothed and cheered his heart to see 300 Catholic children trained to purity and civilization where eight years ago there were but twelve.[8]

The closing exercises took place on June 29, and the Bishop left on July 1.

The summers were always busy, as many children remained at St. Peter's. The Sisters took them on picnics and camping trips. They loved to picnic in the canyon and camp by the Dearborn River.[9]

Early in July Father Cataldo arrived with Father Joseph Bandini. On July 18 water was turned on in the new building which was nearing completion. Father Dols, "Montana's great builder," and the pastor of Great Falls, also arrived for a visit.

The second religious profession at St. Peter's was held on September 8, 1891. Sisters Caecelia Wiegand, Agnes Dunn and Mary Rose Galvin pronounced their vows. A group was also clothed in the Ursuline habit: Sisters Zita Chance, Monica Martin, Tecla Flood, Philomena Gelkins, Scholastic O'Sullivan and Paula Slevin.

Sister Caecelia, (Julia Wiegand) was one of the early boarders at the academy. She was the daughter of George Wiegand who had come West. Julia, at the age of two, came with her mother to join her father at Sun River in 1870. Mr. Wiegand had established a brewery there but later took up ranching near Cascade. A mountain near the family ranch was named Mount Caecelia. When Julia came to the Mission to enter the Ursuline Order, she rode double on horseback with

St. Peters Mission School. Boys' and Priests' residence. Old mission in background, church and school.

her little brother, so that he could return home with the horse. The day was July 16, 1887.

Mary Dunn (Sister Agnes) was a graduate of the Ursuline Academy in Cleveland, Ohio. She came to Montana and entered as a postulant at Miles City on September 29, 1887. She later became a teacher and an administrator.

Mary Rose Galvin (Sister Mary Rose) graduated from the Ursuline Academy at Toledo, Ohio, and came to Montana in 1888. She entered the Order at St. Peter's on July 31 of that same year. She was a gifted teacher, and in 1908, founded the Ursuline Academy in Moscow, Idaho.

The year 1891 brought changes to St. Peter's Mission. Father Joseph Damiani, the superior who had welcomed Mother Amadeus on October 30, 1884, left on June 29 for the Piegan mission of Holy Family. In his place came Father Francis Andreis who was not so understanding of the hardships of the Mission and the interests of the Sisters. During this same year, Mother Amadeus left for Holy Family Mission on November 22 and did not return to St. Peter's until the following year.

This was also the year that the exodus from the log cabins of the Sisters to the new stone house began. The estimated cost of their new building at St. Peter's was $18,000 but it no doubt cost much more. Mr. Nicholas Monshausen was the architect-contractor. Much of the quarry work was done by Mr. James Burns, Mr. John Mannix and hired stone cutters. The carpentry seems to have been under the supervision of Mr. Swanson.

The project was financed by donations, mainly money furnished by Miss Katharine Drexel (later Mother Katharine) and from the family of Mother Angela Lincoln. From February, 1888 until May, 1893, Mother Katharine gave $21,300 and the Lincoln family from February, 1891 to July, 1893, gave $10,500. Bishop Brondel contributed substantial sums from time to time.[10]

Materials from the surrounding hills and neighborhood were used in the construction. The sandstone was quarried in the hills north of the site. (Remains of the quarry can still be seen.) The steps were of granite taken from Square Butte in the Judith Basin. The building was a three-storied structure

Academy

which provided space for chapel, classrooms, art room, conservatory, parlours, dormitories, and refectories for the Nuns and children.

It was still unfinished on December 28, 1891, when Bishop Brondel arrived and announced his intention of remaining at the Mission until they moved into the new house. The annalist recorded:

On December 20 at the head of a broom brigade, His Lordship begins the cleaning of the new house. We and the carpenters are at work all day. The chapel was prepared for Mass and readied for the blessing which was to take place the following day. On January 1, Mass was offered at 7:00 A.M. After breakfast the children greeted the Bishop and he responded in a fatherly way, telling them that of all spots on earth, he preferred to be at St. Peter's Mission.

At two o'clock the blessing of the house took place. The Bishop, with Father Bandini and Father Schuler were met at the Father's house by a procession of Indian and white children, the Nuns and friends, which proceeded over the bridge to the new house. Crossing the threshold, all intoned the psalm, *"Pax huic Domini et omnibus habitantibus in ea,"*[11] and went first to the chapel. The bishop, priests and Nuns then proceeded through all the rooms.

The following days were filled with plans for the great move, and the 7th of January was the date set. At an early hour three teams belonging to Mr. Moran, Mr. Lewis, and Mr. Senecal, drove up. Several other neighbors came to help. Mrs. Senecal prepared and served a dinner to all the helpers. All in all, it was a pleasant day.

On January 8 a dear friend of the Nuns, Mrs. Lemlin, died. She had made her home with them for a year.

School was opened in the new building by Bishop Brondel on Monday, January 11, 1892. The classrooms were provided with slate boards and maps. There was rejoicing over the Bolton hot water heater and the twelve stoves for warmth. All this seemed munificent. Still, there was no floor in the basement, but the thoughtful Bishop made the Nuns a present of a rough board floor before he left.

The annalist writes:

> The chapel has no ornaments save its magnificent proportions. Four large windows give us early and late a view of the wilderness; an old abandoned piano is our altar. It bears an oblong cake box with huge iron hinges for tabernacle, two vases and lilies — a gift — four candles, that is all. An old organ that groans out the sweet song of our prayerful hearts, a small stove that strives to keep us warm, a wood box, a holy water font, a statue of Our Lady.

The Bishop remained until January 14. Mother Amadeus, who had been away since November, returned on February 5.

On March 11, 1892, the annalist recorded, "We have had much suffering of late. Yesterday there was nothing in the house but corn meal — no butter, eggs, syrup, not a drop of coal oil or a bit of money. It is the opening of our seventh year in Montana. Mother says, 'Seven years of famine.' " Two days later, "The illness at the Fathers' was alarming. Father F. Andreis and the Scholastic, Father Bruchet, and 30 boys were ill with pneumonia."[12]

The following day the Nuns left their classrooms and went over to the Fathers' house to nurse the sick. Dr. Francis Adams, a pioneer physician, drove the 35 miles from Great Falls to help. He told the anxious ones that the scholastic was in grave danger. Father Cataldo, the Superior of the Missions of the Northwest, arrived and his first care was to anoint Father Bruchet. All prayed for the recovery of the missionaries.

That evening Brother Schloir was attacked by pneumonia. The doctor, on his second visit, found him in grave danger. Such trials are difficult to imagine, but more were to come. Dr. Adams found a malignant case of diphtheria among the boys. This meant isolation in one of the log cabins. Sister St. Martha and Sister Scholastica were quarantined with the child to care for him.

Father Schuler was away from the Mission, visiting his surrounding stations. He became ill at Sun River, and word was sent that he was dying. Father Cataldo went immediately to see him, and all rejoiced on his return with the news that Father Schuler was recovering. Good Mrs. Healy of Sun River at the "crossing" had nursed him back to health.

Other Jesuits, Father d'Aste and Father Monroe, came to help in the crisis. Father Eberschweiler came from St. Pauls and helped with the Easter services.

In 1886, Father Peter Prando and Father Urban Grassi, S.J., selected a site for a Mission among the Crows on a small creek called Rotten Grass. In February, 1887, the two Jesuits and Eddie Dillon left Helena to build this mission. Their only habitation was a large tent that served for chapel, sleeping, living quarters and kitchen. With help of funds from benefactors, especially the Misses Drexel of Philadelphia, they were able to build a school and a house for the Sisters by the fall of 1887. Sister Magdalen Cox, Sister Joseph of Tiffin, Sister Gertrude of Youngstown, Ohio, and Sister Rose Miller opened school there in October.

In 1892 two more missions were opened. One, St. Charles Borromeo, at Pryor on the Crow Reservation, was intended for the Indians in that region, many of whom belonged to Chief Plenty Coups' band. On February 8 Mother St. Thomas Stoeckle, Sister Agnes Dunn, and Sister Brown left St. Peter's with Father Joseph Bandini to open the new school. The beginning was difficult with a small number of Indians. More Nuns were sent but the attendance was never predictable. It became a saying among the old missionaries in later years when work was heavy and laborers few, "Oh, for the days of Pryor where there were seven Nuns and five girls!"

A request came for teachers from Jocko where the Salish Flathead Agency was located. At long last Chief Charlo had consented to move from the Bitterroot to that part of the reservation. He had held out against great odds, declaring that the treaty between the government and his tribe was fraudulent. The new school was to accommodate the children of this band and was called St. John Berchmans. The Sisters — Mother Angela Lincoln and Sister Amrhein — left on April 19 to start school but found on arrival that the building was not ready. Mother Angela, therefore, returned to St. Peter's and Sister Amrhein went to St. Ignatius Mission.

85

[1] *Letter*, Bishop Brondel to Mother Amadeus, July 9, 1884. Archives, Great Falls.

[2] Howard, *Strange Empire*, pp. 352-356.

[3] *Letter*, Mother Amadeus to Father Lindesmith. Ursuline Archives.

[4] This hotel was on the east side of Dearborn by the crossing and just below the graveyard on the opposite bank. The chimney and stones were still standing in the 1930's.

[5] Houck, *The Church in Northern Ohio and in the Diocese of Cleveland from 1740 to 1890*, 4th ed., 1890.

[6] The Great Northern Railroad reached Harlem, September 13, 1887.

[7] Sister Clotilde Angela McBride, *Ursulines of the West*, pp. 48, 52.

[8] *Ursuline Annals*, Vol. 2.

[9] The Dearborn was named by Lewis and Clark after the Secretary of the Navy.

[10] *Accounts*, St. Peter's, 1884-1893.

[11] "Peace be to this house and to all who shall dwell therein."

[12] *Annals*, St. Peter's, vol. 3, Ms.

CHAPTER 6

"Seven Years of 'Not So' Plenty"
From the Annals

(1892)

April 10 —

Palm Sunday. Rev. Father Munroe distributed palms and left for Benton.

April 11 —

Rev. F. Eberschweiler S.J., our dear old Toledo friend came from Harlem to help us through. We ate tonight off an old table sent as a gift from the abandoned military post, Fort Shaw.

April 14 —

Holy Thursday. Mass at eight by Father Eberschweiler in the old log Mission Church. He trained the Novices who sang the first two Lamentations at *Tenebrae*. Rev. F. Eberschweiler sang the third.

April 17 —

Easter! Snow. Visits from neighborhood— Blessing of the Father's house. We are exceedingly rejoiced to find the Fathers well and at the altar again.

May 2 —

Sr. Angela returned from Arlee Mission which is not to be opened for a month or so. Sr. Ambrnein remained at St. Ignatius. Rev. F. Andreis, S.J., also returned. He had been at Great Falls attending the blessing of Father Dols' new church.

May 4 —

Ex-Governor Leslie paid a flying visit.

May 5 —

Ex-Governor Leslie left expressing his wonder at the beauty and work accomplished at the dear Mission.

May 7 —

About 8 A.M., the bake house burst into a blaze. Today's batch of bread was burned to cinders as well as 3 sacks of flour. We spent a happy day with Mother. She was giving us lessons on the sewing machine.

May 8 —

Thirteen of our girls and three boys made their First Communion. Four postulants who arrived last Friday: Misses Kearns, Dolan, Seery and Fleshman took the cap and cape just before Mass. Two of our children, Cecile Blackfoot and Mary Rose Swan, very low— the latter with something like cerebral trouble.

May 9 —

Today brought the long expected Supervisor Parker—the keen edge was worn off the excitement by the increased illness of sweet little Mary Rose Swan. Her breath of life slowly went out between eight and nine. Her parents came from the Dearborn. We were obliged to sit up as we had given our bedding to the Indian children. Mother having been disappointed of blankets ordered in Chicago.

May 10 —

Mr. Parker began the inspection at the Fathers. At 1½ Mother met him, Father Andreis and Mr. Markham at the head of our stately stone steps. He proceeded to the platform—of the two school rooms on the west side of the house. The children greeted him with a patriotic song and an address in elegant form, to this he responded promising to speak again. Then the quartette sang Concone's "Evening Hymn." Mother conducted Mr. Parker into the Chart and Primer School. In the higher room Mr. Parker was amazed by the reading, writing, spelling, arithmetic and physiology of the children. The next thing on the program was the sewing room. Here twelve dear girls ran as many sewing machines with vim and speed bespeaking skill. This seemed to amaze and delight the Supervisor. Here his amazement went beyond bounds. He could not believe his eyes. The carving especially delighted him. He said it was the first work of the kind attempted at any Indian School. Inspector Parker proceeded to the Study Hall. Here another address awaited him and a National Song. To this he responded simply and kindly. In the parlor, he partook of cake and wine and listened to Sr. St. Paula's voice and the strains of Mother's harp. Then he walked through the house. Formerly an architect he was amazed by its beauty, unfinished though it be. He promises to assist Mother, seems delighted. Says he will obtain 400 pupils for us and will make this a graduating school from the other missions, as it is the only non-reservation school in Montana. From here Mr. Parker visited the workshops, carpenters, shoemakers, and blacksmiths.

May 11 —

Mr. Parker left this morning.

May 13 —

Mother starts for Piegan with Mertie Hickey. She is to remain a day at the Northern Mission and meet Mother Francis at Harlem. Placid death of our neophyte Xavier.

May 16 —

Little Martini Berger herself asks for the Viaticum. At a quarter to twelve she died peacefully.

May 17 —

Dear Mother Francis left for St. Paul's Mission this morning with Sr. Kearns. They hope to

May 22 —

meet Mother at Harlem taking her with them to St. Paul's for a week.

This morning we had the procession of the Rogation Days.

May 24 —

Mass at 6½ and proceed then in line to the fields that skirt Damiani, *"Christus regit Christus vincit, Christus defendat nos."* Father Munroe spent last night and left the Mission this morning.

May 25 —

The last Rogation Procession this morning.

May 31 —

Rev. H. Schuler sang the first High Mass for us in our little Chapel.

June 1 —

La Framboise came from Assiniboine asking for their girls. They were persuaded to leave them until the end of the year. Mr. Trudeau of Choteau left his two little girls, Lucy and Nellie, 6 and 8. Blackfeet ½ breeds, baptized by Father Prando.

June 2 —

La Framboise returned and took his girls. Mr. Lewis brings us ten sacks of potatoes making up 4060 in all with what we bought last month.

June 9 —

Our Mother returns. Bushy Head comes too to see Agessa, and Dr. Gordon of Great Falls.

June 16 —

We walked over to the Mission Church. Nature was alive and joyous. As we returned a red bird perched upon the bridge, and gave us a chery greeting.

June 19 —

Corpus Christi. The procession began after ten o'clock Mass in the usual order. It was a cloudy day with high winds. Eighteen of our dear Indian girls strewed flowers whilst seven walked behind singing *"Pange Lingua"* with plaintive sweetness. Altars were erected at the door of the Fathers' new house and at ours and here Benediction was offered for the first time.

June 20 —

Agessa much better. Bushy Head and his wife left this morning.

June 21 —

Today 21 of our girls made their First Communion. Sixteen being from the dear Indian school. It was a beautiful day. The children wore pink dresses embroidered with white, white veils and green wreaths. They walked to the Mission church for 7 o'clock Mass singing a hymn of joyous expectation— two of Mother's own. Gataya and Eliza Azure were among the communicants, Mary Landry too and Ida Sanborn. While Father was speaking the Mission bell began to toll the death of little Joe Barrow of Dearborn, one of the Fathers' boys.

June 28 —

We sat up until midnight making the children's new pillow slips and cutting out their sheets. At length the task was finished and the new blankets being brought down from the attic, each child was laid away between two white sheets, a new pillow under her head. The dormitory is a beautiful sight. Pillow slips of bright blue, bright red blankets, snowy white sheets on each bed. This latter is quite an unusual luxury in an Indian Mission and one the Nuns themselves do not enjoy.

June 30 —

The closing exercises were very successfully rendered in the two white girls' school room. The Indian girls gave "Miracle of the Roses," the white girls "King Rene's Daughter," freely adapted to school room recitation. The boys under the unmatched leadership of Mr. Markham, S.J., came off with colors flying.

They outdid themselves in the little incident of "Gen. Gage and the Boston Boys." A violent, very violent rainstorm burst out during the exercises. We missed our Bishop. Mr. Mannix of Augusta and Mr. J. Douching of Belt with the Morans, Lewis and all our neighbors attended.

July 1 —

First day of vacation. All received a formal visit from Rev. Sansone, S.J. He was accompanied by Bro. Schloir, S.J., Mr. Bruchert, S.J. and Rev. F. Andreis, S.J. Agessa at midnight peacefully passed away.

July 2 —

Mother's birthday.

July 3 —

Agessa was buried today. We had high Mass of Requiem. Itathan (Ursula), Francesca Bathnay, Immaculata Watzinitha all of the Gros Ventre and Rose Isca of the kindred tribe of Assiniboines clad in white with wreaths of orange blossoms acted her pallbearers. It was very eloquent. Philomena St. Dennis, a Cree ¼ breed, entered Little Adelaide Jackson, Rosalia La Framboise and the Landrys with the two little Belgardes left for a spell.

July 4 —

Mr. James Burns was paid in full of all demands and left the mission after working here many years.

July 5 —

We began making more sheets for the girls' beds.

July 7 —

Mr. Allis of Great Falls came over to see his children. Toward nine in the evening, the dense cloud and odor of smoke alarmed us. The danger was traced to the Bolton heater— the soot took fire in the pipes. Mr. Mosney, our hired man, and Mary Fields arrived on the scene of action and by throwing salt on the fire and turning the hose on the chimney and heated wall saved this beautiful house.

July 12 —

The passenger train runs through Cascade to Wolf Creek the first since the heavy rains of just one month ago June 11.

July 13 —

Our evenings are spent weeding and bugging in the potato patches. Arrival of Father Dols.

July 16 —

Messrs. Moran and Laura Trands, "the Mothers" came today.

July 21 —

Dr. Newman examined the children and left by stage. We prayed for good news and lived all day in its expectation, but we were answered by no bad news, which is good news nowadays.

July 24 —

Mother received a fine cow in part payment for the Farrell children's board.

July 25 —

Father Dols arrived. He is going out to the boys' picnic to fish.

July 31 —

Miss Whitfield our carving teacher left. Her contract closed on July 1st. Mother held a powwow with the Gros Ventre Indians.

Aug. 4 —

We went out on a picnic to Trout Creek, and brought back twenty-five fish.

Aug. 5 —

The Gros Ventre Indians came again.

Aug. 6 —

Miss Ella Galvin appeared from Toledo to visit her sister, Sr. Mary Rose.

Aug. 9 —

His Lordship arrived this evening on business.

Aug. 10 —

His Lordship left this morning.

Aug. 12 —

Miss Kate McAndrews arrived from Hermon, Pa.,

to assume the cap and sweet duties of the missionary life.

Aug. 14 —

Our Indian girls looked lovely in fresh pink dresses and white sun bonnets with small blue dots.

Aug. 15 —

The children sang a new Mass but Mother abolished the choir wishing to substitute congregational singing. Rev. Rebman, S.J., Rector of St. Ignatius Mission, arrived and opened our annual retreat.

Aug. 23 —

Srs. Seery and Fleshman left for Pryor Creek Mission. We were unspeakably rejoiced and grateful to hear that St. Peter's contract is renewal for 180 children.

Aug. 27 —

Srs. Casey and Laurentia returned from the Crows.

Sept. 2 —

Dear Mother left this morning taking Srs. Laurentia, McDonald and Essie Prenderville to open the house at Arlee. Srs. Seraphine, Berchmans, Moffitt and Rossie Bunt left for St. Paul's Mission.

Sept. 4 —

Allie and Maggie Moran entered Cecile and Josephine Falcon for the Indian School.

Sept. 5 —

Miss Mary Ryan entered to take the cap. We were overjoyed to have our dear Sister Antonina's Sister.

Sept. 6 —

The entire Ford family came to spend the night. Anna Keogh is to be married in the morning to J. Ford.

Sept. 7 —

Married from our Mission Church, Anna Keogh and Joe Ford. They came over to breakfast.

94

Sept. 9 —

John Mosney and Mary Fields touched rifles at each other, but there was no firing. We hired George Mosney today at $1.00 a day and another hand at $1.25 a day.

Sept. 10 —

Entered Claudia Toole niece of Governor Toole. We enjoyed a visit from Rev. Fathers T. Tosi and Van Gorp. The former kept us spellbound with tales of the strange land and clime. Entered the Indian School, Delarth, Mary, Justine Landry of Augusta. Our friends Mr. Lewis and Moran hauled hay for us this afternoon. We have put in 18 loads.

Sept. 16 —

Miss Ryan with Emma McLaughlin and Jessie Bushnell left for the Piegan Mission.

Sept. 23 —

Arrival of Bishop, Rose Wohlgemuth from Boston. Misses Wohlegemuth and Curran take the cap.

Sept. 25 —

Arrival of Miss Nellie Brown from Savannah. His Lordship confirmed some twenty of the mission children. Promptly at two o'clock the *"O Gloriosa Domina"* resounded triumphant in the log cabin church and Misses Dolan and Amrhein, Lanbutry and Casey, Flaherty and Briel, Kenney and Moffet, Schweelzer and Brown, H. Adams and C. Adams entered and took rank in the sanctuary. The ceremony proceeded peacefully and with all the unction of the tenderest devotion. After the ceremony the new novices visited the Bishop and the Fathers at their house.

Sept. 26 —

Departure of His Lordship.

Sept. 28 —

Sr. Wohlegemuth left for St. Ignatius with Addie Buchanan.

Sept. 29 —

Sr. Curran left for Piegan with Aimee Auger. Miss Belle Browne takes the cap.

Oct. 5 —

Dear Mother left us this morning for a long missionary tour. We received a note from her at Cascade. She was bound for Harlem.

Oct. 7 —

The teachers from Fort Shaw Government School visited our school and seemed well pleased. Mary Fields freighting. The Nuns made the best of the opportunity to rid out the old laundry. They burned rubbish but amid were some cartridges. They went off and shot Sr. St. Gertrude very near the eye.

Oct. 8 —

D. Keiley entered.

Oct. 12 —

An Emerson piano came today. A dispatch from Mother to send Srs. St. Monica and St. Philomena to St. Ignatius Mission.

Oct. 14 —

Mr. Madden was killed Thursday by being thrown from his buggy. Our two novices saw his corpse on their way to Cascade.

Oct. 15 —

Miss Rosecrans arrived.

Oct. 16 —

Mr. Madden burried at High Mass.

Oct. 19 —

This morning Miss Rosecrans returned to Helena. Her stay has been to her a source of pleasure and profit.

Oct. 21 —

Today we celebrated the 400th anniversary of the Discovery of America by a play, "Christopher Columbus," enacted by the Indian girls. They had a fine time at a picnic on Mt. Ursula with songs and patriot odes.

Oct. 23 —

Srs. St. Catherine, Lucia and Angela drove to

Sun River and Fort Shaw to beg Dr. Newman to draw Sr. St. Catherine's tooth. He refused, not having the necessary forceps. On returning Mary Fields who drove the nuns lost her way and the nuns were lost on the prairie. Reaching the foot of Crown Butte they called at a cabin which chanced to be Mr. Farrell's. This gentleman who was recently married to Miss Whitefield jumped on the box and drove the grateful nuns home.

Oct. 25 —

Sisters Angela and St. Catherine went to Great Falls to have the latter's tooth extracted. They were most kindly entertained by the Sisters of Providence who are just settled at their new "Columbus Hospital."

Oct. 27 —

We heard today that Dorchester and his wife are at Fort Shaw.

Oct. 28 —

At a general sewing here we began a set of pretty bed spreads for the Indian girls.

Oct. 30 —

Mr. Moran sent us a present of $50 to get something for our chapel for the cure of his daughter, Nora.

Nov. 5 —

Mable Mannix and Kate Kavanagh and two Miss Barrys entered.

Nov. 10 —

We lighted a coal fire in the furnace tonight the first in St. Peter's Mission. It is to be delivered at Cascade for $5.50 a ton. It is good hard coal.

Nov. 14 —

At about ten o'clock Daniel Dorchester reached the Mission. He went to the Fathers' first and came over to the Convent at about 2:10. He expressed himself much pleased. He returned to Cascade about 4 P.M.

Nov. 17 —

The dear Sisters in the washhouse suffered much from the cold today. In dampening the clothes the water was frozen on their fingers.

Nov. 18 —

A letter from Sister Irene tells us that Mother is at the Blackfoot Agency getting children for St. Peter's Mission.

Nov. 19 —

Tonight Father Superior Damiani returned after a long and painful absence of a year and a half.

Nov. 20 —

Today we had the visit of our long absent Superior—the dear Indian girls greeted him with songs, address and the play "Columbus"—after its close two played a duet. Watzinitha and Mary Wallace and Annie Evans played alone on the piano to Father Superior's intense surprise. The white girls also addressed and sang.

Nov. 28 —

The door opened and our dear Sr. Zita entered. She and Sr. Santa Clara arrived after being on the way since Wednesday the 23rd. On the night of Saturday the 26th they knocked at the door of two of our old friends who refused them admission. That night the dear imitators of the travelers of Bethlehem spent the night out on the prairie in the black cold of Montana's November—wind and snow. The house that refused them shelter was the very next night burned to the ground. They saw it burn. They brought us 15 Blackfeet girls: Lizzie Big Eyes, pure Blackfoot, Ursula Cutbank, pure Blackfoot, Josephine Wetherwax, half breed, first pupil received by the Nuns who opened the Blackfoot Mission, Mary Jane Hazlett, one of the first, Josephine Hazlett, sold for two ponies to a Chinaman, received by the Agent and given to Mother, Anne Howard adopted by the Howards, Anne

Brown, surnamed Cleveland, Susan Russell (father) butcher at the Agency, Mary La-hiche, Nancy Burd who spent 5 years at Carlisle, Emmia Croft, Rose Upham, for the White School, Isabel Bear Chief who is traveling with Mother, Alice Aubrey for the White School, Lucy Aubrey for the White School.

Nov. 29 —

Father Schuler started for Blackfoot.

Nov. 30 —

Father Superior left this morning. He took with him Bro. Galdos and Mr. Markham. This latter is bringing Blackfoot boys to the Mission.

Dec. 3 —

Mother returned.

Dec. 5 —

A letter from "Rittenhouse Square" Tabernacle Society informs us that we are to have a ciborium.

Dec. 7 —

A photographer from Helena took views of our house and our children for Rev. L. B. Palladino, S.J.'s work, *The History of the Church in Montana.* He took the house, a pretty group of girls at the sewing machines, the Indian girls *en masse*, the White girls, the Community Nuns teaching the Indian child-ren carving, drawing, painting and embroid-ery, harp, mandolin, guitar, piano. Our Mother sat in the midst teaching catechism to "Big Eyes."

Dec. 8 —

The photographer came over in the afternoon and took some single pictures as also a pretty group, "The Novices at Recreation" in which Mother was the central figure. We were surprised in the evening by the arrival of the photographer, Mr. Moriarty of Helena, with Rev. F. G. Andreis, S.J., and asked to hear the music he had painted. We spent a pleasant musical evening. The gentleman is somewhat of a musician. He has taken most of his pictures by the bright flash of the "Magnesium" light.

Dec. 10 —

Tonight we received a bundle from the Tabernacle Society of Rittenhouse Square, Philadelphia. We opened it with grateful hearts— Mother found a beautiful little silver ciborium.

Dec. 12 —

Francesca Sleeping Bear and Susie Lard ran away at night prayer time.

Dec. 13 —

They had spent the night in the hay stack of Morris's horse ranch and were returned to us by one of the hands. Mary Fields shot an eagle in the wing and brought it to us as a trophy.

Dec. 15 —

Srs. Seraphine and Berchmans returned from St. Paul's Mission. They missed the stage, hired a conveyance, were thrown in the snow and reached here only at 8 P.M.

Dec. 19 —

Father Schuler returned bringing with him 11 boys and 3 girls from Lewistown.

Dec. 20 —

Amid this intense cold Sr. Seraphine with Mary Wells for her companion started for the new Arlee Mission.

Dec. 21 —

The Sisters in the washhouse stood in two feet of snow and the water dripping from the hot water tanks froze on the floor.

Dec. 24 —

We enjoyed the privilege of Midnight Mass in our little chapel.

Dec. 25 —

Christmas day. We had the mass of the Aurora at

100

9 A.M. by Rev. F. Schuler and at 10 the high Mass in church by the same Father. At 8 P.M. our children had their Xmas tree and we closed the blessed day in Thanksgiving.

Dec. 31 —

The last day of the year closes cold and snowy. From the Tabernacle Society of Washington a most welcome gift, three vestments, a ciborium, an incense box and censer and a most beautiful ostensorium. This last was a gift from a lady in New York who wishes her name to be kept secret. We are beginning the year '93 without a cent of money in the treasury but with the charity of our members more closely knitted together.

1893

Jan. 1 —

We open a new year.

Jan. 2 —

Mother very ill.

Jan. 4 —

Mother began to teach the children dressmaking.

Jan. 5 —

Mother continued her lessons in spite of her illness.

Jan. 6 —

The weather is unusually mild.

Jan. 8 —

The Fathers invited us over to a Xmas Tree.

Jan. 10 —

Our dear neighbors, Messrs. Moran, Lewis and Tabor, brought us a load of coal. Father Markham brought nine Piegan boys and two girls, Maggie Rose and Cecile Russell.

Jan. 11 —

This evening the dear Indian girls invited Mother and the Nuns to an entertainment. Mary Wallace and Watzenitha played a duet, "Petit Carousel" and Watzenitha played alone,

"Blue Bells of Scotland," Annie Evans played the "Five Finger March" and "Gallop." We were amazed as they have been taking lessons only since June.

Jan. 14 —

Sisters St. Patricia and Agatha left this morning for the Crow Mission.

Jan. 17 —

The Sacristan is putting down matting—a gift of Mr. M.C. Galvin of Toledo in the Chapel.

Jan. 20 —

Sister St. Berchmans received the news of her father's death.

Jan. 23 —

Mother Mary of the Angels left for St. Paul's Mission taking with her the novice, Sr. St. Gertrude.

Jan. 28 —

Mother receives a present of the works of Gilmar Shea in the original edition. Mother prizes them deeply.

Jan. 30 —

Mother was taken very ill after Mass and was confined to her cell.

Jan. 31 —

We are suffering intense cold and are short of wood. Thermometer in a shelter marked minus 39° and in Helena minus 52°.

St. Peter's in winter.

Feb. 1 —

Our wood pile is going down and no one is willing to go into the mountains to hew it. Mother gathers all the girls into one room, both White and Indian, and all the Nuns into another in order to save our scant fuel.

Feb. 4 —

The Indian girls finished hemming and making 400 towels for their own use.

Feb. 8 —

Today Bro. Schloir was called in to see Gataya who was supposed to be very ill. He pronounced her case incipient typhoid fever and the child was quarantined in the visitors' room and Sr. St. Catherine appointed to watch over her.

Feb. 9 —

The Indian girls went out sliding on the pond. Gataya out of danger; has not typhoid fever.

Feb. 10 —

Today the Father's chimney caught fire and Father Markham who was sent to extinguish it came running over here to inquire where our fire was. Sr. St. Anna told him the fire was in his own house. Mother St. Ignatius returned today from St. Paul's Mission. Mother bought Lemire's wagon for the purpose of bringing Nuns back and forth.

Feb. 13 —

Tonight Sr. Seraphine returned from Arlee Mission.

Feb. 14 —

Mother St. Ignatius went out with the Novices to carry wood and was overcome by the wind. We had supper in the Art Room. Sr. Seraphine got the ring out of the pancakes.

Feb. 16 —

Today Mother St. Ignatius, Srs. Berchmans and St. Lucia started off for the Piegan Mission. They went in the big wagon and four-horse team and enveloped in their red blankets they resembled Indians starting off on a long trip.

Feb. 19 —

Tea Brown left. Mrs. Brown gave Mother a present of 12 hens.

Feb. 21 —

Mr. C.B. Toole, brother of the ex-governor, called to see his daughter Claudia.[1] He was much pleased with the music we gave him.

Feb. 22 —

The boys entertained us with a bright little entertainment in honor of Washington's Birthday. Mr. Toole left.

Feb. 24 —

Father Andreis and Bro. Bartz sick. We go over to cook.

March 1 —

Mr. Moriarty, the photographer, came up to retake the photographs of the boys which had proved a failure.

March 4 —

Whilst we were at Benediction in Church Sr. St. Agnes accompanied by Mother St. Thomas returned from Pryor Creek.

March 7 —

Sr. St. Genevieve very ill.

March 10 —

What was our surprise to see our beloved Bishop standing beside the road side. He had arrived with Very Rev. J. M. Cataldo, S.J. Mother and the Fathers mutually agree the one not to remove, the others not to dismiss, Sisters except during vacation.

March 13 —

Father Cataldo spoke to the Community and Novitiate in general and to some in particular. This great missionary announced his intention of going to Alaska.

March 14 —

This morning His Lordship and Very Rev. J. M. Cataldo, S.J., left. Father Andreis went with them to Helena.

March 18 —

Tonight at Benediction we sang Bro. John's Litany.

March 19 —

We had a new organ today in Church and Bros. John's organ was taken away.

March 21 —

Today the picture of Our Lady of Prompt Succor was suspended under St. Peter.

April 1 —

Bright and joyous Easter. Both Masses in Church.

April 5 —

We are milking 31 cows and feeding 21 calves. Sr. St. Scholastica with 5 girls does the milking.

April 6 —

Sr. Seraphine returned from Helena. She reached there with Sr. M. Columba on Easter Sunday night who was anointed that night by Father Palladino.

April 8 —

We were unspeakably rejoiced by the return of our beloved Mother. Mother brought with her Mother St. Ignatius and left Sr. St. Agnes as Superior at the Blackfoot Mission.

April 12 —

Busy preparations for Mother's departure.

July 15 —

Mrs. Slevin and Martha Slevin arrived from St. Louis to visit their daughter Sr. Paula.

July 21-30 —

Annual Retreat by Rev. J. Neri, S.J., of San Francisco.

Aug. 5 —

Father Van Gorp, S.J., who has recently been appointed Superior General of Rocky Mountain Missions paid his first official visit to our Mission.

Aug. 25 —

At 2 the doctor came. Dr. Gordon of Great

Falls, with his young wife, says Sr. Veronica may live two weeks—may live two months.

Sept. 4 —

Mother returned.

Sept. 6 —

Our Bishop came up this evening.

Sept. 8 —

Sister Veronica pronounced her vows. The Cleves arrived from Boston. They are friends of Sr. St. Elizabeth.

Sept. 11 —

Sr. Stanislaus of Bedford Park who had come here for her health left yesterday for Miles City and St. Labre's. Mr. and Mrs. Mannix left today leaving us Mable and Clarence.

Sept. 13 —

Thirty-three children came with Father Schuler from Lewistown. Twenty-two boys, eleven girls entered in the Indian School.

Sept. 18 —

Today Sisters Xavier, Bernard, Esperance, and Clara with Lettie Foley went to St. Ignatius Mission. Father Rebman reached here from St. Ignatius Mission. A wagonload of children reached here from Depuyer. Four were girls.

Sept. 19 —

Father Rebman our new Superior visited us today.

Sept. 20 —

Father Andreis asked for music in the evening. Sister Elizabeth sang "Bridge," Lindsey, Sr. Genevieve played "Tarantelle," Hiller, Sister Carmen played List's "XII Rhapsodie", Sister Paula sang Braga's "Angel Serenade" in Italian accompanied by Sister Carmen's violin obligato. This last delighted our good Father.

Sept. 21 —

Father Andreis[2] said Mass and took breakfast. We all saw him off and he gave a parting blessing. Mr. and Mrs. Cleves with Mary and Emma Amrhein left us for Boston. Mr. Cleves gave Mother a present of new coal stoves.

Sept. 22 —

This evening Father Van Gorp, S.J., Superior General of the Indian Missions arrived.

Sept. 23 —

This morning the new Superior General of the Rocky Mountain Indian Missions, Very Rev. L. Van Gorp, S.J., said Mass in our little chapel. At two, he with Fathers Rebman and Sasia visited the house. . . .Father Sasia is appointed by the new general of the Jesuits Visitor General. He will go to Rome to report on the state of the Missions.

Sept. 26 —

We had a visit from Father Van Den Heuvel, the new Young Dutch priest stationed at Lewistown.

Sept. 28 —

The Novices went out for a picnic.

Sept. 29 —

Mr. Moran gave us a load of beautiful potatoes.

Sept. 30 —

We spent the day pulling up stones and mending the boys' clothes.

Oct. 2 —

Mother St. Felix left us to be Superior of Piegan.

Oct. 3 —

Arrival of Srs. Berchmans and M. Teresa from Piegan. Later still in the evening we were surprised by the arrival of Srs. Bernard, Antonia, Eugenia, Monica, Philomena, Wohlgemuth, Dorsey and McDonald from St. Ignatius.

Oct. 5 —

This morning Sr. Ignatius and Eugenia went to Arlee. Sr. Teresa accompanied them there where she is to be met by Sr. Marguerite and proceed to St. Ignatius.

Oct. 8 —

This morning Father gave us Mass in our Chapel

at 7. In the evening we greeted him as Superior of the Mission.

Oct. 11 —

Isabelle Bearchief, Emma Croff, Susie Smith and the two Goberts came from Piegan and entered the Indian school.

Oct. 14 —

Srs. St. Tecla and Fleshman returned from Pryor Creek Mission.

Oct. 16 —

Sr. St. Berchmans returned to San Antonio. Mr. Moran from the World's Fair, Father Schuler from his missionary tour.

Oct. 17 —

Today Miss Krieger entered the White School.

Oct. 20 —

Sr. Mary Rose went to Great Falls this morning to have her teeth attended to. She took Lily Allis to the doctor.

Mother quite ill. Sr. Mary Rose returned form Great Falls, but left Lily Allis at the hospital. The child is threatened with loss of her eyes from scrofula. Today Mother engaged Robert Loss to go on the "Round Up" at $1.00 a day for us.

Oct. 28 —

Father Rebman sent us half a hog he had slaughtered.

Oct. 30 —

Nine years ago today this Mission and Novitiate were opened. Since then have entered and been clothed here: Srs. Marguerite and Helena, Cecilia, Agnes, M. Rose, Terese, Antonia, Zita, Monica, Thecla, Veronica, Philomena, Scholastica, Paula, Marian, Gertrude, Patricia, Genevieve, Catherine, Elizabeth, M. Columba (dismissed), Rosalia, Agatha, Colette (dismissed), Lucia and Anna.

Oct. 31 —

Since her return Sept. 4th Mother has been

confined to her room but today she came back to us. M. Assistant returned tonight from Piegan with Josephine Wetherwax. In spite of her poverty Mother bought a few apples and the children enjoyed the customary "ducking."

Nov. 9 —

The little Joe Bush children returned. We get paid but for 90 and our attempt to have the contract raised failed.

Nov. 11 —

Mr. Kimer, 107 Grand Street, Helena, came to do dentistry.

Nov. 13 —

Feast of St. Stanislaus—Mother had been promising the Novices a day with them and in order to greet her they prepared and executed the following program:
Vision of St. Stanislaus—Sr. Carmencita, "The Old Church Tower," Vocal Quartette, Sopranos: Srs. St. Thecla and Paula, Alto: Sr. Carmencita, Tenor: Sr. St. Elizabeth, Bass: Sr. St. Genevieve. Heaven's Gate Tours, Sr. St. Elizabeth, "Blue Bells of Scotland," Farmer, Instrumental Quartette—Violin, Sr. Carmencita, Harp, Sr. Genevieve, Guitar, Sr. St. Paula, Piano, Sr. St. Angela. "Polish Dance," X. Scharwenka—Op. 3 No. I; "Heavens Hath Shed a Tear," Kucken—Sr. St. Paula, Obligato, Sr. Carmencita, "Hymn to St. Stanislaus," The Quartette.

Nov. 23 —

The children went for a sleigh ride.

Nov. 24 —

The children's sleigh broke down yesterday about four miles from the Mission. Some walked on ahead and sought shelter from the cold at Mr. Moran's. Others, the laggards, were met by Mr. Lewis who mended their sleigh and sent them home. Mr. Moran kept our children all night and sent them home this morning after a fine breakfast.

Nov. 26 —

About seven P.M. Father Rebman arrived. In alighting from his buggy he stepped on a snow bank and was thrown on to the wheels. His eyes were badly cut by the frame of his glasses.

Nov. 27 —

Mary Fields returned today. She spent last night in a snowdrift about ½ way between here and Cascade and walked all night to keep from freezing.

Nov. 28 —

Mr. Moran kindly sent us a present of five chickens for our Xmas dinner.

Nov. 29 —

Sr. Berchmans from the Cheyenne Mission arrived.

Nov. 30 —

At ten o'clock a magnificent display startled our snow cloud sky—the sun dogs.

Dec. 3 —

We had very high winds. The two Sisters from Quebec were blown down on their way to High Mass and Sister St. Monica was twice laid prostrate. The dust was blinding. Tonight Mother received a present of 96 yards of carpet.

Dec. 5 —

This morning Miss Curran, who has spent a year in the missions, left and returned to New York.

Dec. 7 —

A letter came from the Bishop allowing Miss Helen Sheble to take the cap and enter the

Novitiate. Father Rebman has very generously allowed us the use of his horsepower to
saw our wood.

Dec. 8 —

Miss Sheble took the cap this evening.

Dec. 9 —

The missing freight from Quebec arrived at last
and we saw oil paintings of Mother Mary of
the Incarnation, Mother St. Joseph and Madame de la Peltrie in our humble convent.

Dec. 11 —

The pipes were frozen in the basement; at
suppertime the pipes burst.

Dec. 18 —

Sr. St. Zita dismissed.

Dec. 20 —

Sr. St. Genevieve left today with Anne Brown
for the Holy Family Mission where she is to
play and head the chorus during the holidays,
Mother St. Felix having sprained her wrist.

Dec. 24 —

A new sanctuary lamp which Miss Cleve of
Boston sent us; as we began office our dearest
Mother lighted the new lamp. This night the
Solemn Office of Nativity was sung at St.
Peter's Mission for the first time. At 11½
P.M. we walked over in the cold moonlight to
the Church where we had low Mass with
hymns and violin accompaniment from Sister
Carmen Dunne.

Dec. 25 —

Xmas Day Masses at 6½ and 7 in our chapel.
High Mass at 10 in Church.

1894

Jan. 1 —

Mr. Markham went today to the hospital in
Helena. Father Rebman paid us a New Year's
visit. Mother is very ill.

Jan. 8 —

Mother Mary of the Angels went to Helena to

consult a doctor, taking Gataya for her companion, who is threatened with tumor on her eye.

Jan. 9 —

High winds. This morning when Father opened the Chapel door the wind swept the vestments, vases and candlesticks off the altar.

Jan. 10 —

We hear that Mr. Markham is ordered to Spokane.

Jan. 13 —

Today ten years ago Mother left Toledo for Montana. "Old Gray" is dying. We are sorry to lose this relic—the first gift of Father Damiani to Mother.

Jan. 16 —

Old Gray died today.

Jan. 18 —

Miss Sarah A. Chance (Sister St. Zita) left.

Jan. 21 —

Profession of Sisters St. Monica, Thecla, Philomena, Scholastica and Paula. Clothing of Sisters: Dorsey as Sr. St. Eulalia, Fleshman as Sr. St. Rita, McDonald as Sr. St. Barbara, Wohlgemuth as Sr. St. Hildegarde and Carmencita Dunne as Sr. Annunciata.

Jan. 22 —

Sisters Sts. Monica and Thecla left this morning for the Cheyenne Mission. Mr. Markham returned from the hospital in Helena.

Jan. 24 —

This morning the Bishop left.

Jan. 30 —

Sr. Elizabeth of Quebec with Sister St. Sebastian and the Novices Sr. St. Eulalia and Barbara left this morning for Holy Family Mission. We received some altar goods from the Sisters of Notre Dame in Cincinnati.

Jan. 31 —

The two young novices, Sisters Hildegarde and Rita, left this morning with Flora San

113

Sauveur for St. Paul's Mission.

Feb. 4 —

Cash so much worse that Mother sends for Dr. Adams.

Feb. 6 —

Dr. Adams arrived with Mr. Allis.

Feb. 7 —

This morning at 12½ A.M. little Cash Allis peacefully breathed his last. Sister Veronica died. It was just three o'clock. She died in the 22nd year of her age and the 5th month of her religious profession.

Feb. 8 —

Today little Cash Allis was buried.

Feb. 10 —

At 9 o'clock Rev. J. Rebman sang High Mass and spoke a few touching words on the merits of our little Novice. After the rite Messrs. Lewis, Moran, Gilole carried the remains to our new graveyard.

Feb. 12 —

Today Dr. Adams came and did up Sister Thomas' legs in plaster of Paris bandages.

Feb. 15 —

Our dear Father Damiani appeared tonight with Father Sardi of San Francisco.

Feb. 19 —

Our dear Superior left this morning with Father Sardi. Maud Allis ran away for fear of punishment but was caught and brought home. Sr. Genevieve had one hand frozen when on the search.

Feb. 20 —

Today Sr. St. Bernard and Mary of the Angels went to Helena to consult the doctor. The latter will not return. Father Superior Damiani has asked for her as Superior of his mission. We received from Boulogne-sur-Mer a banner of St. Ursula and two vestments, one white, the other green.

114

Feb. 23 —

Sister B. Sacrament arrived from Miles City.

Feb. 24 —

Miss Lent of Philadelphia arrived to take the cap. Srs. Mehegan, Brown, Ryan and Catherine arrived from Holy Family Mission.

Feb. 28 —

Mother was summoned to St. Ignatius Mission ....Sr. Catherine accompanied her.

March 2 —

Sr. Thomas went to Great Falls Hospital with Martha Brown. Mr. Moran drove them down. We sent Mr. Moran a cake for his birthday.

March 18 —

At eleven this morning Atathan died.

March 20 —

Atathan was buried today. Heavy snow and intense cold.

March 24 —

Letters from Mother. Sister B. Sacrament is appointed to accompany Sr. Pelagia to Pryor Creek. Sister Scholastica and Sister Lent ordered to the Crows.

March 25 —

Easter Day, very stormy.

April 9 —

Today Mother returned with Sister Thomas.

April 13 —

No mail. News was brought that the Great Northern R. R. is on a strike and that there can be no traffic for 30 days.

April 18 —

Today our neighbor, Mr. John Brown, visited us and made Mother a gift of 100 trees. Messrs Houghton and Gorman of Cascade also called and cleaned and tuned our organ and piano.

April 20 —

Today the old time coach began to run again between Great Falls and Helena. They stopped for dinner at the Mission. We thus had 20 unexpected guests. Among them were two Sisters of Providence, Mother Provincial, Sister Julian, formerly of Benton and Sr. Joseph of Arimathea, Superior of Benton Hospital. This is the first time we have ever had Sisters for our guests. Mother presided in the kitchen while the novices entertained the company with music.

April 24 —

Mr. Flinn, having gone to Great Falls, brought us back the mail arrested there by the strike.

April 29 —

First Communion Sunday, 42 children.

May 2 —

The strike comes to an end and trains ran again, as usual. One night brings over 1,000 letters.

May 8 —

On this day we had a clothing in Church. The ceremony was performed by Rev. J. Rebman, S.J., the Bishop having delegated to him his authority. Sister Seery became Sr. St. Philippa, Sister Kelly became Sr. St. Juliana, Sister Sheble became Sr. de Merici, Sister Kearns became Sr. St. Justina, Sister Mehegan became Sr. St. Christina, Sister Ryan became Sr. Mary Josephine and Sister Brown became Sr. Dolores.

May 19 —

His Lordship today arrived.

Bishop John B. Brondel at St. Peter's.

May 21 —

Sister Mary Rose who has long been ailing today went to Helena to consult Dr. Treacy; Sr. Bernard accompanied her to consult the oculist.

May 25 —

The Bishop also left today. Sr. Bernard returned but the doctor has ordered Sr. M. Rose to remain at the hospital.

May 26 —

Busy preparation for the Corpus Christi Procession. . .Little trees were planted on either side of the carriage walk up to the house and the gateway was arched over with evergreen. Mail brought our dear Father Superior and Fathers Rebman and Cataldo.

May 27 —

The procession pronounced the most beautiful the Mission has ever beheld. At 9 High Mass followed by a sermon was offered by Father Cataldo. Then the most devout procession filed out of the log cabin Church. First the cross bearer, then the girls, the women, the boys, men, Nuns, choir, the dais and our Blessed Lord. This was carried by Bro. Francis, Messrs. Lewis, Morgan and McDonald. Father Rebman carried the Blessed Sacrament. Fathers Damiani and Schuler were deacons and Fathers Nicholson and Cataldo censer-bearers. The long file wended all the way from the cabins to our home through the long line of already planted trees. We sang hymns all the way.

May 28 —

Little Baby Ducharme enters. Visits from Fathers Cataldo and Damiani. Present of a second chalice from Rev. A. Sanvadet and organ from Rev. Father Peter.

May 30 —

Sister Mary Rose returns from Helena.

June 3 —

A violent hailstorm. Margaret Getts made her First Communion and left.

June 4 —

Mrs. Lawyer Walsh[3] arrived with her little daughter and her friend, Mrs. Denham.

June 5 —

Our cattle rounded up into the corral numbered 133 head. The Visitors had a picnic in the canyon.

June 16 —

Mother and Sr. Mary Rose left for Piegan Missions.

June 21 —

Icie Rolls and Dollie Getts, Della Collins and Mary Boniface made their First Communion.

June 25-26 —

Very successful examination in White and Indian School.

June 28 —

Miss Power, Emma Wells, Miss McNulty, Mrs. Cummings with Marguerite Cummings, Mr. and Mrs. Mannix came to assist at the closing.

June 29 —

Very successful closing. Mother with Sr. Mary Rose returned.

June 30 —

Little Catherine Landry died.

July 2 —

Father Peter's organ came during supper.

July 4 —

The children went off on a picnic.

July 12 —

Mr. Moran invited the Nuns and white girls to his house for a picnic. We spent the day on the porch of his home and in the shade of his pretty trees.

July 14 —

Sister Mary went to Great Falls to have her felon lanced. She has not eaten or slept for three

119

nights and days. Sr. Paula was her traveling companion, whose throat is to be treated.

July 24 —

Today Mrs. Flinn, her children and her sister-in-law, Miss Lucy Flinn, arrived to pay us a visit.

July 25 —

Mother left today for Great Falls.

July 26 —

Our guests took dinner with Mrs. Moran and came over to a musicale in the evening. The Moran family also came.

July 27 —

The Flinns left this morning. Mary Fields went with them. The Bishop has ordered that she be dismissed from the Mission.

July 28 —

Letters from Mother ordered Sr. Philomena to Holy Family and Srs. M. Rose and Josephine to Helena.

July 29 —

Mr. Wiegand took dinner here and at 1 P.M. started off with our buggy and his team for the Holy Family Mission whither he conducted Sisters Thomas, Bernard and Philomena. At 7½ we were enjoying a quiet recreation when the ominous cry "Fire" filled us with consternation. Under the (sacristy) stand was a box of candles and a box of benediction charcoal. A spark must have fallen into the box for when we entered the sacristy, the stand, the sacristy cupboard, and the chapel wall were ablaze. Father Schuler who was taking his recreation on the porch of the Fathers' house saw the fire pouring out of the sacristy window and gave the alarm. The men from Lemire's and Bros. Barty rushed to the rescue. We turned on the hose and in ¼ of an hour the fire was out.

Aug. 4 —

Miss Ella Galvin arrived also. Mr. Heileman, the Superintendent of all the Indian Schools,

120

Mrs. Heileman and Dr. Winslow, Superintendent of Fort Shaw. . . .They inspected the whole house. . .were delighted with the water power, bathing arrangements and school room appliances. . . .After the visit they took dinner and enjoyed a varied entertainment.

Aug. 6 —

Mrs. Dawson arrived bringing her adopted child, Lorena Young, to school.

Aug. 7 —

Whilst the young professed Nuns had gone off on a picnic Nancy Burd died suddenly of a hemorrhage at 6 P.M. Sisters Moore and B. Sacrament arrived from the Crow Mission.

Aug. 9 —

Lawyer and Mrs. Brady arrived.

Aug. 10 —

We had a musical today for Mr. and Mrs. Brady.

Aug. 11 —

Our guests go out driving. At about 3 o'clock a fearful cloudburst and hailstorm assailed Mother on her way from Cascade.

Aug. 14 —

The mail wagon brought Sisters Marguerite and Dorothea with little Caroline from St. Ignatius Mission.

Aug. 15 —

On this day our little Hilda Dunne, Mother's youngest niece, who had been one year in the Academy, took the cap.

Aug. 17 —

Mr. Wiegand comes to spend a little time with Sister St. Cecilia.

Aug. 25 —

Father Neri, S.J., from San Francisco reached here.

Aug. 27 --

Opening of annual retreat.

Aug. 31 —

Miss Ella Galvin, who has been visiting her sister, Sr. M. Rose, left for Toledo.

121

Sept. 4 —

Little Mary Larance died today.

Sept. 6 —

Little Mary Larance buried today.

Sept. 12 —

Clara Wiegand and Mr. Lary married today in the log church. Wedding breakfast in the Convent.

Sept. 24 —

Mother Mary of the Angels, with Sisters Agnes, Irene, Philippa and Justina left in our buggy for Holy Family Mission. Sr. St. Cecilia and Dolores left for Arlee Mission and Sisters Seraphin, Berchmans and Dorothea for St. Ignatius Mission.

Sept. 26 —

Sr. St. Clara left for Pryor Creek and Sister Marguerite to take charge of St. Labre's Mission.

Oct. 2 —

Sister St. Charles, a professed Nun from Ursuline Convent, Tulline, France, accompanied by Mlle. Massart from St. Omer, reached here today.

Oct. 7 —

Mother gave the cap to Miss Baldwin and Miss Massart.

Oct. 24 —

Feast of the Angel Raphael brought us Miss Mary Lenihan. She came to us all the way from California. . .and asked permission to take the cap. Six years ago she made her First Communion here. She is the first boarder to enter the Novitiate.

Oct. 30 —

Today the 10th anniversary of Mother's coming to St. Peter's Mission. Mr. Moran loaned Mother $500.00 without interest. *10 years— nine houses—74 Ursulines.* We celebrated by setting out the flowers and planting the garden given us by Father Sanvadet of Lorain, Ohio.

Oct. 31 —

Mr. Moran gave us a barrel of apples.

Nov. 1 —

Mother received from Mrs. Lewis a root that helps her.

Nov. 11 —

Today Lawyer Brady and his wife arrive from Great Falls.

Nov. 12 —

Mr. Brady took photographs of the Novices elect and several of the Nuns and children.

Nov. 13 —

On this day Srs. Marianne, Gertrude, Genevieve and Elizabeth pronounced their blessed vows. Lawyer and Mrs. Brady, Father Dols, and our neighbors honored the ceremony by their presence. Sisters McVey, Lent, Hilda and Octavia received the Holy Habit. The Bishop preached on the occasion and Mr. Adams, S.J., brother to Sister Gertrude and Sister St. Marianne, wore the surplice for the first time acting as sub-deacon.

Nov. 23 —

Our dear friends, Messrs. Moran and Lewis, are hauling for us our winter inlay of flour.

Nov. 28 —

Mother left this morning to consult the Bishop in Helena about matters at Pryor Creek. It may be that Mother will have to push on into the Yellowstone Valley.

Nov. 30 —

Mother and Sister Mary go to Billings.

Dec. 3 —

Mother on this day reached Pryor Creek Mission.

Dec. 4 —

Mother removed Sister Pelagia from her charge of the Pryor Creek Mission and left Sister Scholastica in her place.

Mother was anxious to reach Billings before dark. This the driver promised to do on condition that the party leave the Mission at noon. He proposed reaching the new bridge over the Yellowstone about 5 P.M., which on the night was to be completed. Mission matters detained Mother. The party, consisting of Mother, Sisters Pelagia, Clara and Mary drove off from Pryor Creek at 1 P.M. The journey began prosperously enough. They were in a new surry, drawn by two splendid horses in a harness used only for the second time. At 6½ minus 5 min., Mother had previously looked at her watch, the driver entered Blue Creek, an arm of the Yellowstone, at the old crossing. He was making for the new bridge which that day was just completed. Suddenly Mother was awakened by a shrill cry from Sister Mary "Mother, look, we are drowned." The water had reached to Sister Mary's neck. Mother was plunged in to her shoulders. Large blocks of ice floated down the rapid current. The horses with ears cocked, necks stretched to the utmost, barely kept their lips out of water. At this ghastly scene, the driver fainted. This was the Mercy Stroke of Divine Providence. Had he preserved consciousness and urged them on they would have dashed into the abyss dug by a water spout the preceding Spring. About an hour before Mother had given the Nuns' valises to Brother Carfagno who followed them with the trunks. Our four victims cried out, "Sacred Heart of Jesus! Save us!" Mother promised the Sacred Heart to do something great if they were rescued. Had the horses moved a step, they would have perished. Mother saw that while they were motionless the Nuns were safe. Looking about, she noted the fact that they were not too far from shallow water for the driver to climb the mud-fenders and reach the shore. Rousing him from his faint, she directed his movements and told him when ashore to take one of Brothers' horses and ride back to the nearest human habitation, a cowboy's shack two miles away. This was accordingly done. On reaching this spot he entered and fell mute and senseless on the threshold. Perceiving some danger they at length roused him sufficiently to say, "Nuns in the River."

These brave men rode at once to the rescue and with all the gallantry and deep respect of honest American hearts lifted the Nuns out of their watery grave. Raised as it was on a half inverted position on the brink of a chasm, every move in the surrey exposed the occupants to the danger of imminent death. But this was nothing to our Mother's heart. She lifted out the sisters one by one, Sisters Mary, Clara, Pelagia, climbing over Mother and the back of the inverted seat on to branches and logs which the cowboys extended to rescue the Nuns. In this way they reached shallow water and waded ashore. It was five minutes before 6½ when they entered the abyss; it was ten minutes past seven when they emerged, the peril having lasted 3/4 of an hour. The silent stars had crept out to witness the ghostly scene of mercy and of peril.

It was very cold. . . .To escape freezing they ran about gathering branches and built a huge fire. At a distance of four feet the moisture rose in steam from their dripping garments in front and icicles clung to them from the back. At length they were driven to the shack of the cowboys who had saved them so gallantly. These brave and truly courteous men vacated their poor home for the Nuns and spent the night out-of-doors, beside a huge camp fire endeavoring to dry the soaking wraps. It was two hours before the horses could be rescued from the stream. The next morning it was found upon investigation that these poor creatures had been standing with their forefeet on the verge of the cavern dug by the water spout the preceding spring and that their hind legs had been swimming in the stream. All morning the men spent fishing wraps from the stream and piling brick at the treacherous crossing to give warning of the danger. The county, they said, should be sued for neglecting to mark the dangerous spots. At one P.M. the following day, Mother and her party forded Blue Creek at the proper crossing and reached the Yellowstone in safety and passed over the bridge completed the night before.[4]

*   *   *

1895

Jan. 1 —

The first day of the New Year. Dr. Adams came from the Falls. He renewed Dr. Treacy's assertion that Sister M. Rose should go South. Fr. Rebman paid us a visit of greeting and announced the arrival of Fr. Palladino's book. We spent the evening looking over and enjoying the book, *Indians and White in the Northwest* and eating the fine apples sent by Mr. D. Morgan of Helena.

Jan. 5 —

The men hauling the safe could not get home yesterday. Help was sent this morning but they were obliged to leave it at a distance of five miles from here.

Jan. 7 —

Mother went to Cascade accompanied by Sister Eugenia who is to undergo very serious treatment in the Great Falls Hospital; Big Eyes and Watzinitha who are to be operated on, and Emma Croff who is to be Mother's companion to Holy Family Mission. When Mother reached Cascade it was 20° below zero.

Jan. 8 —

Today, the Nuns guided by Mr. Swanstrom pulled up to 2400 lb. safe from the foot of the front steps to Mother's door. It was obtained for us second-hand by Lawyer Brady of Great Falls.

Jan. 14 —

Later Saturday night the 12th Mother reached Blackfoot. She feared to take the drive to the Mission. During the night a violent chill and fever overtook her and she was confined to bed, in the house of Joe Kipp at Blackfoot, his squaw waiting upon Mother. Our good friend, Joe Kipp, rode off some place and managed to find somewhere 36 gr. of quinine. On Monday, dear Mother wrote us a slight account and proceeded to the Mission.

Jan. 21 —

Today Mother passed through Cascade enroute to Helena to attend the Jubilee Celebration of the Sisters of Charity. But the train was wrecked! The engine rushed off the track and poor Mother did not reach Helena till Tuesday morning at 1 A.M.

Jan. 23 —

Dear Mother returned.

Jan. 26 —

News from Great Falls assures us of Sr. Eugenia's steady improvement.

Feb. 15 —

At 4½ this morning our little pupil Theresa Lewis, aged 15 years, breathed her last. She was surrounded by her family and dear Mr. Moran. At about nine this good friend brought in the sad news.

Feb. 17 —

This morning little Theresa Lewis' remains were brought to our Chapel. Her mother, father, sisters, Mr. Tabor and children followed the remains. Mother, Nuns and children met the remains at the door. The Mass was sung by Father Rebman, S.J. The funeral services were conducted by Father Schuler, S.J.

March 7 —

Today seven years ago Mother received her first Indian pupils at the Mission—eleven Blackfoot girls of whom Rosada, still with us, was the baby.

March 11 —

Sr. Gertrude and Sr. Baldwin left to replace Sisters Tecla and Monica at the Cheyenne Mission and Sr. Philippa went with them to Cascade with A. Youke. The latter are to go

127

to St. Ignatius Mission.

March 24 —

Mother's desire to go to Alaska increases every day.

March 29 —

We gathered together at 8 A.M. to wish our dear Superior a happy feast.

March 31 —

Mother went into the kitchen and sent over refreshments to the Fathers. Each boy received a cake, a ball of popcorn and 1 orange, a hot roll and a little butter ball.

April 12 —

We set up in the parlor the book case Mother received as a feast day present, thus beginning the nucleus of a library at the Ursuline Convent of St. Peter's.

April 14 —

Heavy snow ushers in our Easter Day. Mr. and Mrs. Rowles, Mr. and Mrs. Ferrel of Sun River, Mr. and Mrs. Moran and Leo Debruc came to give Mother their Easter Greetings. The Novices entertained them with music and elocution.

April 18 —

Dodie Sanborn is taken with an acute attack of erysipelas.

April 23 —

On this day in 1876 our dear Mother Superior in Toledo was administered "Sugar of Lead" instead of salts. The doctors succeeded by strong antidotes in saving her life but they burned out the coating of her stomach.

April 26 —

Little Philomena Berger made her First Communion. Father Rebman, though ill, left for Great Falls to replace Father Dols.

April 29 —

Father Schuler called to Sun River. Father Rebman returned bringing with him Miss

Kiernan from New York who is to take the cap.

May 2 —

Ursula was buried today. Ursula was about 16, of the Blackfoot tribe. John Cutbank and Paul, Ursula's brothers, came with Mrs. Upham and Mertie Upham to see Ursula. They received the three letters together at Kipps' on Monday the day of the child's death whereas the first letter had been written to inform them of her illness.

May 6 —

Mr. and Mrs. Curly Head and Mrs. Walls came to see their children. They pitched their tents close at hand.

May 8 —

Little Philomena Berger died at 2 P.M. at the hospital in Great Falls.

May 9 —

This morning the Gros Ventre Indians went off to Great Falls to see Dodie. Mother offered to let (one of the men) guide them but they indignantly refused saying, "We do not wish to travel with half breeds."

May 11 —

James Tabor was buried this afternoon.

May 13 —

Little Maggie Lewis returned to school and entered the First Communion class.

May 17 —

Father Rebman left for Great Falls where he is to assist Father Dols.

May 20 —

Mother had the two upper stories of the house smoked with sulphur today.

May 23 —

Feast of the Ascension. The First Communicants were 21 in number among them Margaret Moran, Margaret Lewis, Lorena Young, Elizabeth Rowles.

May 29 —

Brother O'Hare ordered to Alaska.

June 6 —

We all went with Mother to see the chapel and to hear her plans for the painting of the chapel. Mr. Hubert, a French fresco painter residing at Philipsburg, is here to do the ceiling.

June 8 —

Snow 4 ft. on the level at the Missouri.

June 10 —

Mr. A. P. Flanigan from Miles City, one of Mother's earliest acquaintances there, called here on his way to Anaconda. He was accompanied by Mr. Herman.

June 15 —

Mr. Hubert, the fresco painter of Philipsburg whom Mr. Hull hired to paint the Chapel ceiling, left today.

June 16 —

Corpus Christi procession.

June 26 —

Father Prando came here to make his retreat before going to the Blackfoot Mission whither he has been transferred.

June 27 —

Today Mr. and Mrs. Amrhein, Mrs. Rusec, Marguerite Rusec and A. Amrhein reached here today to visit Sr. St. Elizabeth.

June 28 —

Our Bishop arrived today for his Episcopal visit. He came over to visit the Nuns and told us of the honor that had greeted him at Notre Dame. In the evening the boys performed, "St. Sebastian" for the Bishop and the Amrheins and Mother held a rehearsal of our commencement in the log house.[5]

June 29 —

At nine A.M. the Bishop said Mass in the Church and confirmed the children. Among the

130

group were 26 girls. In the afternoon the closing exercises were conducted in the unfinished log cabin. Among the guests were Dr. Winslow, 2 teachers and 4 employees who came from Fort Shaw, Mrs. Flinn, Mrs. Roberts, our neighbors and quantities of people. The hall was very crowded.

June 30 —

The Bishop said Mass in our Chapel at 7½. At High Mass the Bishop preached in French. In the afternoon we had another visit from His Lordship and in the evening he sat with us on the front steps.

July 1 —

The Bishop began his Episcopal Visitation.

July 2 —

The Bishop this day promises us a school at Great Falls.

July 3 —

Today we enjoyed an early visit from Father Prando.

July 4 —

Independence Day was celebrated by a visit from Father Prando, S.J. who showed us some photographs of Indian life and gave us each one.

July 5 —

Dora Keiley and Isla Silvers left this morning.

July 6 —

Mother today received the first wool spun and carded at St. Paul's Mission. The banns of Mary Wells and Joseph Gump, the Fathers' foreman, were called today for the first time.

July 8 —

Last night we had a concert in honor of our guests—Mr. and Mrs. Amrhein and Mrs. Reiser.

July 9 —

Our dear Mother was awakened by an early message by telephone—the first that crossed

131

our line—a blessing from the Bishop at Helana. Bear Chief came to get Isabel and Anne Evans.

July 10 —

Today Mrs. Weatherwax came for Josephine. Bear Chief went through the house and expressed his delight. When shown the paintings of the girls, he said: "Ah, the Gros Ventre girls don't do well as the Piegans." He never, before, he said, had seen anything so beautiful as the house and our chapel.

July 11 —

Today Mr. Pepion came with his new little wife, "Jessie Whiteman." He took with him his two dear girls and Anne Evans.

July 13 —

The Nuns spent the day in the fields weeding and killing potato bugs.

July 15 —

Mr. J. Shepherd called with M.D. Fortune, Dr. F. Cooper, the 2 Miss Downings, Miss Thurman, Miss Newman, Miss Richardson, five lovely girls, who are spending a few days with Mr. Cooper.

July 18 —

Today, Mother and all of us with the children held our annual picnic at Mr. Moran's.

July 19—

Opening of our annual retreat, Rev. P. P. Prando, S.J.

July 20 —

Sr. Margaret brought Mary and Anna Seilnacht, the former for the Novitiate, the latter for the boarding school.

July 23 —

Fire broke out in the washhouse at about 10 A.M. Blankets and comforts near the chimney in the upper room were found smouldering. Mary Wells was married to Mr. Gump. They were married in Church but had breakfast here.

132

Buffalo run near St. Peter's. 75 foot drop.

July 28 —

Father Prando has impressed us with his sanctity. We have never missed an annual retreat and always the full 8 days.

July 29 —

In the evening Mother gave the cap to Mary Seilnacht.

Aug. 1 —

Mrs. McDonald, wife of the proprietor of the Grand Hotel in Great Falls, and Mrs. Putnam, wife of the Catholic contractor of that city, dropped in on us and asked permission to stay a few days. We entertained them with music after supper.

Aug. 5 —

Mother St. Magdalen leaves today for Toledo.

Aug. 6 —

Visit from Lawyer and Mrs. Downing of the Falls. We entertained them and showed them the Chapel. Their little girls, Isobel and Bessie, whispered to their Mother on leaving, "Mother, we would like to be Nuns." M. Magdalen left the Crows today alone for Toledo.

Aug. 10 —

Sr. M. Rose left for the Crow Mission.

Aug. 17 —

Today Supervisor Moss arrived. He went through the house, examined the children's art work, carving, painting, sewing, plain and fancy work, studied the plan of the school in detail, listened to the Sister's music. . .the bathing and water supply delighted him.

Aug. 22 —

Letter from St. Ignatius announces Sr. Berchmans' departure.

Aug. 25 —

Visit of Lieutenant Ryan, U.S.A., who passed

through making a topographical map of the section.

Aug. 26 —

Srs. Holy Angels and Angela leave for Toledo.

Aug. 27 —

We hear today that Sr. St. Ignatius leaves for Toledo.

Aug. 28 —

Mother left for St. Paul's Mission accompanied by Sister St. Charles and Francesca Bathay who returns to her people.

Sept. 4 —

All the potato stalks frozen to the ground. Mrs. Ferris brought her two daughters.

Sept. 5 —

Mrs. Ferris left this morning at 6 leaving her two daughters, Pearl and Edna Hendren, in the White School.

Sept. 7 —

Mother passed through Cascade on her way to St. Ignatius.

Sept. 9 —

School began today. Our neighbors began hauling our flour, Messrs Dubus and Tourneary bringing 6,000 lbs. Miss Nellie O'Brien of Dedham, Mass., arrived to take the cap. Our dear friends, Messrs. Moran and Lewis, brought us 4,000 lbs. of flour.

Sept. 13 —

Messrs. Moran and Gump bring the last of our flour. Father Van Gorp arrived.

Sept. 15 —

Father Rebman received word that 30 children from Lewistown were in Great Falls awaiting transportation to the Mission.

Sept. 17 —

Today 15 girls arrived and Christine and Mary Gardner from "Gild Edge." These dear girls were for many years at St. Paul's Mission. One of the little girls from Lewistown is a deaf mute.

Sept. 20 —

Srs. Lutegarde and Regina left for St. Ignatius.

Sept. 21 —

Mother reached home.

Sept. 25 —

Threshers were at work.

Oct. 3 —

Mother this day left our Mission for a one month absence. Just before leaving she gave the cap to Miss Nellie O'Brien.

Oct. 7 —

Sisters Massart and Charles left for France at 11 A.M.

Oct. 16 —

Srs. Camilla and Defrosia (Sisters of Providence) were advised to come up from Cascade—pleasant and sisterly visit.

Nov. 21 —

Mother had to stop over night at Little Browns'; blinding snow storm.

Nov. 22 —

Sr. Seilnacht was clothed and took the name of Sr. Gonzaga.

Dec. 1 —

Reaching Cascade, Mother received a dispatch from Rev. J. Damiani telling her to hasten to Holy Family where Sr. Angela was dangerously ill.

Dec. 25 —

Mother has sent us two angels swinging censers which we placed beside the crib.

Dec. 31 —

Last day of the year Mother still at Piegan. We call this year, the year of departures.

*   *   *

1896

Jan. 1 —

Mr. Moran called with New Year's greetings.

Jan. 2 —

Clear and cold.

Jan. 3 —

27°. Mr. Moran and family came to receive Holy Communion in spite of intense cold.

Jan. 7 —

Mr. Moran told us he remembers a change of 105 degrees in the temperature taking place within 24 hours at the Mission.

Jan. 14 —

We begin to cut ice.

Jan. 16 —

Men cut blocks of ice 16 in. square.

Jan. 18 —

Chinook blows.

Jan. 19 —

Mother left Holy Family. Sr. Joseph, local Superior at Miles City, left for Cleveland.

Jan. 22 —

The mail wagon drove up bringing a form muffled in buffalo robes. It proved to be Mother.

Jan. 23 —

Mother erected the statue of the "Secret Heart of Jesus Pleading," put in place the Nun's *prie-dieu* and children's benches. At a little before five, Mother walked out the chapel door, down to the buggy, and drove off to the Crow Mission.[6]

Jan. 30 —

Eddie Ford very sick from pneumonia. Father came and telephoned Dr. Sweat who drove right up to the Mission and expressed grave apprehension.

Feb. 1 —

High Mass of Requiem followed by interment of little Eddie Ford.

Feb. 17 —

The children took walks and made taffy.

Feb. 24 —

A crazy man was about yesterday shooting at random. The bullet whizzed by our dear

137

Nuns as they came from Benediction, and the Fathers' men went out to apprehend him. Mr. Gorn, an old friend of the Mission, died yesterday with all the rites of the Church.

March 4 —

We sent Mr. Moran a cake and birthday greetings.

March 5 —

Mr. Moran took all our children sleighriding.

March 9 —

Sr. Catherine drove to Great Falls with Gataya, Dodie, Big Eyes and A. Brown for medical treatment. We here thought Sr. Annunciata too ought to go, so the six left with her and Mrs. Gump at 9½ A.M.; a distance of about seven miles the buggy broke and Mr. Gump returned for instructions. He took the big wagon and they continued their journey.

March 12 —

On this day our dear children were stricken down with measles.

March 15 —

Mary Fields today celebrates her 64th birthday. . .We sent her a birthday cake.

March 19 —

Flora Amrhein taken with typhoid fever.

March 23 —

At 7 A.M. after a night of suffering little Lilly Allis died.

March 24 —

Lilly Allis was buried from the Church this morning at 8 A.M.

April 5 —

Easter Sunday—bright with spiritual joy.

April 6 —

Our dear children all went out on a picnic.

April 13 —

Sr. M. Rose went to Great Falls with Gataya and Little Clara.

April 22 —

Today the Bishop reached here and came over to

138

spend the evening recreation with us.

April 23 —

Bishop visited house and inquired into the plans of Srs. Anna, Rosalia, Patricia and Callista. After seeing them he left orders that they should be dismissed as soon as possible.

April 28 —

Word from Mother orders Srs. de Merici and Genevieve to Miles City.

May 6 —

News from Miles City reports poor Sr. Genevieve much worse. The Church there burned down.[7]

May 12 —

Today Father Van Gorp reaches the mission.

June 3 —

Martha Brown was married to A. Lemire at 9 A.M. in Church and Nuns and girls attended.

June 6 —

Miss Gertrude Riefourath, who is teaching at St. Peter's District School, came for a piano lesson, and Miss Robinson of Flat Creek School called also and took a lesson on the guitar.

June 7 —

Corpus Christi. A most beautiful procession—the Mission was decked in flags and flowers. The day was a perfect day. The Mission never looked so beautiful. The little Indian girls who strewed flowers wearing pink dresses and white caps and little baskets strung about their necks with pink ribbons. The other Indian girls wore their blue polka dot dresses. Martha Brown Lemire called to give thanks to Mother for the nice wedding cake sent her.

June 8 —

Mr. Surprenant makes us a present of a drop curtain, "Saint Amadeus," for the stage.

June 9 —

Mother returned. The children went out to meet Mother, but so frightened the horses that

139

Mother got out at the schoolhouse and walked home.

June 12 —

First Communion of Big Eyes, our little Blackfoot girl, and 9 other Indian girls. Mother gave us a treat of strawberries.

June 26 —

Boys' Program.

June 27 —

The Bishop arrived.

June 28 —

The Bishop said Mass in our Chapel and after High Mass gave Confirmation to about 30 persons, including our children. At 7 we had our entertainment very successfully before a large audience who came over after for refreshments. Mr. and Mrs. Strain, Dr. and Mrs. Longeway, Lawyer and Mrs. Brady arrived toward evening.

June 29 —

Promptly at 8 the Bishop arrived in our Chapel to profess Sisters Innocent, Catherine and Agatha. The ceremony was beautifully conducted. At 4 P.M., the Indian girls gave "The Vestals." In the intervals the White girls were examined in Arithmetic, Grammar, and Stenography.

July 1 —

Several boarders left and Sr. Elizabeth drove down to Cascade with all of them for a picnic.

July 6 —

On this sad day, Mother received tidings that we have lost our contract. On St. Peter's Day little Annie Barnaby of the kindergarten while out walking with our Nuns was drowned. Mother grieves more over this than over the lost contract.

July 18 —

Toward evening Kate Pambrun drove up with

her little brother James. She was indignant that he had been dropped at Choteau without notifying her. She found he had been wandering around for two days without anything to eat. The Fathers had begun sending the children away and had put this little one on Mr. Goin's wagon with directions to drop him at Choteau. Kate took him to Fort Shaw and Superintendent Winslow offered to keep him on condition she brought him and the girls ...Mother succeeded in keeping them on condition she kept James also. Mother took the latter and gave him in charge of Mr. Hollenback. This little seven-year-old is the nucleus of the boys' school.

July 31 —

Sudden announcement of the death of Mr. Byron Strong. Mrs. Hull came up after Lulu who was sent with one of the Nuns to attend the funeral.

Aug. 5 —

The few boys that had remained were today taken to St. Ignatius.

Aug. 6 —

On this day our last cheque from the government reached us: $1944.00. *"Dominus regit me et nihil mihi derrit."*[8]

Aug. 14 —

Sister Annunciata arrived in Helena to be treated by Dr. Treacy and learn banjo and mandolin which Mrs. Guthrie offered to teach free of charge.

Aug.16 —

Mother left Helena for Great Falls on business with Lawyer Brady.

Aug. 17 —

Incorporation is decided upon and Lawyer Brady draws up Articles for Mother. Mother visits the Black Eagle Falls and Great Falls Smelter.

141

Aug. 22 —

> Father Muset and Sister Annunciata reach our Mission.

Aug. 24 —

> Opening of annual retreat.

Sept. 1 —

> Father Muset gave us Exposition. He came over in the forenoon, gave each a picture, showed us photographs of Alaska and told us his experiences there.

Sept. 5 —

> Father Rebman came over to say his farewell Mass.

Sept. 7 —

> Father Rebman sent us from his storeroom some useful presents. At 12:00 he left for Spokane where he is appointed Procurator.

Sept. 8 —

> Winnie Coleman, niece to our Sister Mary, made her First Communion at eight o'clock Mass.

On July 2, 1895, Bishop Brondel had promised the Sisters a school in Great Falls. The offer was repeated the following year with the hope that each city in his diocese would have an Ursuline Convent.

Mother Amadeus called at the First National Bank on Sept. 16, 1896, and was received by Mr. Mattison, the cashier, and introduced to Mr. Rinker, president of the Great Falls Townside Company. The latter received Mother's request for a grant of land for a new school and promised to notify her when James J. Hill reached the city.

On Sept. 21, Dr. Longeway drove Mother up to Prospect Hill where she was delighted with the beautiful view of the junction of the Sun River with the Missouri. She prayed that God might give her this spot for her academy. Later she took supper at the Fenyan Bakery. The proprietor, Mr. Fenyan, an Austrian, offered his two children as the first pupils of the new school, the first Ursuline convent in Great Falls. Mother consecrated this new institution to the Blessed Virgin naming it "Mary Hill."

When Mother arrived on the third she found that Mr. Hill

142

had gone on to the coast. She went to Lawyer Brady's office and signed the Articles of Corporation for the Order in Montana under the title, "Ursuline Convent of the Holy Family."

Three days later another call came for a meeting. Mother Amadeus had gone to Helena to see the Bishop, but she left at once for Great Falls, meeting Mother Angela and Mother Mary Rose at Cascade. On the train they met Miss Virginia Flanigan who offered herself as a boarder for the school.

The interview finally took place on Oct. 8, with Mr. Hill who promised her a block with alley closed on Prospect Hill. Paris Gibson, father and founder of Great Falls, received Mother's proposition most graciously, and advised her to locate near the park marked out for the city, telling her that he would arrange to have a pipe laid to conduct water from the park to the convent. Mr. O'Hanlon called on Mother at Columbus Hospital and told her he had talked to Mr. Hill about the new foundation.

However, Mother was not given the property she wished, and grieved over the loss and disappointment.

Oct. 18 —

      Sr. Paula left for Cheyenne Mission with Mary Wallace—the former to be in charge, the latter to teach.

Oct. 27 —

      Emma Croff returns and enters the White School.

Oct. 30 —

      Father Bandini, appointed Superior, called. He, Brother Francis, Mother, Sisters Mary and Martha are the only ones here who were here twelve years ago.

Nov. 5 —

      The new stove, "Gold Coin 117," bought by our generous Mother, and the hard coal diffuse heat through Chapel.

Nov. 16 —

      Bishop telephoned saying he could not come to the profession and appointing Father J. Bandini, S.J. his delegate for the occasion.

Nov. 21 —

At 8:30 A.M. the beautiful ceremony of profession began. Sisters Eulalia, Rita, Barbara, Hildegarde, Annunciata, Philippa, de Merici, Amata, Lucia, Justina, M. Josephine, Dolorosa were professed, and Miss O'Connor took the holy habit of Religion and became Sister Fidelis.

Dec. 8 —

Mother today received a letter from Mother Antoinette, Superior of Quebec, saying she had recalled her three Nuns. Some time ago Mother had received the same word from Three Rivers.

Dec. 24 —

Went over to Midnight Mass.

Dec. 25 —

Glad Christmas Day. One of the sweetest and happiest days ever spent at this dear Mission. At 7 A.M. Father Bandini said his three masses in our Chapel.

* * *

1897

Jan. 1 —

Both Masses in Church.

Jan. 6 —

This morning the wind blew the art room curtains up against the hot stove pipe. In an instant they were in a blaze but Sr. Agnes gave the warning and by God's mercy the fire was extinguished without further damage.

Jan. 8 —

A year ago Mother offered herself to Father Tosi, S.J., on the Alaska Mission. He accepted with joy. All things were made ready for our departure when Bishop Brondel refused his permission.

Jan. 20 —

Sr. Cecilia went off to Blackfoot. Sisters Philippa and Catherine to St. Ignatius. Sisters

144

Marguerite and Juliana to St. Paul's. Sisters Gertrude and Barbara to St. Labre's.

Jan. 24 —

It was 40° below zero.

Jan. 30 —

The mail brought Mother a shawl from Margaret Cusack of Brookline, Mass. This dear friend put a "special delivery" stamp on the parcel, thinking it would reach us sooner.

Feb. 2 —

Mother writes to Mother Katharine Drexel begging her help.

Feb. 5 —

Owing to the scarcity of Mistresses the little Indian girls were left in the Art room under the care of one of the Indian girls, Watzinitha. Rose Delamotte, Helen Ducharme, Selma Belgarde, Sadie Pambrun, Jeanie Tarne, and Annie Joupe took "Rough on Rats" which had been spread for the mice. About 15 minutes afterwards this was discovered. Mother and the entire house were in consternation. Warm mustard water was administered. Then Rochelle salts, white of eggs and castor oil with powdered chalk.

Feb. 6 —

The little children are being fed on gruel, milk toast, barley water and bland food. They continue to improve, thanks to God.

Feb. 16 —

Mother Katharine Drexel sent us $750.00 and the promise of supporting 30 girls at $100.00 during the year 1897 if she lives.

Feb. 27 —

Sallie Enright came from Helena to visit Mother. She is a relative of Mother St. Laurence of Youngstown and a pupil of the Ursulines of Toledo.

March 3 —

On this day Father Damiani, S.J., arrived to see Bro. Francis.

145

March 4 —

Mr. Moran—57 years old. Mother sent him a three-story cake.

March 9 —

Father Damiani left today.

March 29 —

Program. What pleased Mother most was to hear herself greeted for the first time in Indian. Louise Pepion spoke in Blackfoot. Aliza Azure spoke in Assiniboine, Jeannie L. Heureux spoke in Cree, Lulu Strong spoke in French and Mary Hollenbach in German. Mother was much pleased with the Delsartian Pantomime, "Paradise and the Peri," from the boarders.

March 30 —

St. Amadeus Day.

April 5 —

Anita Rosecrans arrived for a short visit. Mother saw in the *Bulletin des Missions Catholique* that Father Rene has been appointed Prefect Apostolic of Alaska instead of Father Tosi. Mother wrote to Father Rene and begged him to make it possible for her and a band of Ursulines to devote themselves to the Eskimos of Alaska.

April 20 —

Miss Rosecrans left for Helena.

May 3 —

Gabriel brought Mother a little wolf.

May 9 —

Thirteen little girls made their First Communion. Fire broke out in the Indian girls' infirmary through the flue leading up from the kitchen through a badly plastered hole opening. Mother went up at once and the few Nuns at home soon put out the fire.

May 19 —

Saddie Enright left.

146

May 21 —

Dense smoke at about midday hid Square Butte from our view...The mail man tells us at noon a prairie fire had started two miles this side of Great Falls.

May 31 —

Baby Azure died at 3:15.

June 1 —

The Cheyenne Indians were on the warpath and Mother was most anxious to leave to go to our Nuns there but was detained by Father Bandini's violent opposition to her departure, and the heavy and constant rains. Badger, brother to Lucia, one of our girls at the Cheyenne Mission, murdered Hoover, a sheepherder at Barringer's Ranch. The Whites demanded his surrender, which was finally done by White Bull, the chief. In the interval, much excitement prevailed and all the women were removed from the Reservation. Mother M. Angela telegraphed to Mother that our Nuns were in great danger and Mother spent the interval in great anxiety.

June 10 —

Mr. Howe came from Great Falls some days ago and is busy surveying and staking Mother's claims.

June 20 —

A perfect day; beautiful procession of the Blessed Sacrament.[9]

June 23 —

The fifth volume of our annals begins on this page.

June 24 —

Examination of Music of the Pupils of the Ursuline Convent, St. Peter's Mission.

June 26 —

Lightning and hailstorm. The dams overflowed and threatened to flood the Mission. A muskrat made a hole in the Fathers' dam; the roar and rush of the waters could be heard from Mother's room.

June 28 —

Heavy rains. The Bishop arrived in excellent health and spirits.

June 29 —

St. Peter's Day—Confirmation. The following programs were successfully carried out before large audiences, after which the guests were served supper. The Indian girls gave "St. Lucia," the White girls, "Crown of Glory" and "Paradise and the Peri."

July 2 —

Father Van Gorp bids Mother give up all thought of Alaska and announces the closing of Arlee and St. Labre's, our first Mission.

July 3 —

The photographer, Isah Erikson of White Sulphur, takes a group of our Indian girls with musical instruments and leaves for Augusta.

July 4 —

Father Van Gorp left tonight. . . .He formally announces to Mother that the Jesuits are to be withdrawn from St. Peter's Mission and from Montana unless the Bishop gives them some spot for a College.

On April 29, 1897, Bishop Brondel blessed the church at St. Labrés. He was assisted by Fathers Van der Volden and Van der Pol.

That same day John Hoover was murdered by Whirlwind, Philip Stanley, Hachlayana (Sparrow Hawk), and Little Whirlwind. The Jesuits decided to leave St. Labré's as well as St. Peter's.

In August, Mother Amadeus went to St. Labres determined not to leave this dear Mission among the Cheyennes where the Sisters had suffered so much.

White Bull with his daughter, Margaret, made a solemn call on Mother, Lucia interpreting. White Bull asked how long Mother would keep his children. An instant Mother paused, then looking up to Heaven with the sublime confidence of the Saints, Mother answered, "As long as you will send them, White Bull." The old man was touched, and many (of the Indians present) grasped Mother's hand which he pressed to his lips. Margaret had been Mother's companion when returning the first time from St. Labre's to Miles City. Often they slept together in the same tepee. White Bull had let her come to school on condition that Mother would give her a carpet camp chair which the nuns had brought from Toledo, and which had been Mother Alphonsus'. Today Margaret asked for this chair and Mother gave it to her.[10]

The following day, White Bull gave his photograph as a gift to Mother, showed her letters from George Bird Grinnell and Gen. Miles' picture.

The Jesuits left the Mission on August 10.

At eight, Fathers Van der Velden and Van der Pol came over to bid us goodbye. As we knelt for their blessing, the former said with a voice choked with deep emotion, "Sisters, God bless you for your devotion and the many examples of virtue you have given. I leave our Lord with you. Let that be your consolation. Pray some times for me and I will pray for you. *'Benedicamus,'* etc." We followed the Fathers to their home.

Father Van der Pol begged Mother to have it cleaned and keep for herself whatever she would find in it. He told her also to take the Regulatro and statue of St. Benedict Labré over to the convent.

The last wagonload of freight rolled off drawn by Mr. Ed Yeager and then Fathers Van der Velden and Van der Pol drove off in a buggy. Father Van der Velden had labored here 12 years and rode off today broken in heart and health, begging God to call him soon to Himself.

When we went in to clean his room, we found that his bed for that length of time — winter and summer — had been nothing but a table on which a cow-hide is stretched. He never allowed anyone to enter his

149

room and kept the bed covered with a sheet during the day.[11]

Mother remained at St. Labré's nearly a year. She suffered the deprivation of Mass along with the Nuns until a priest could be obtained. There were occasional visits from Father Van den Broeck of Miles City. Christmas Eve Father J. Vermaat from Holland arrived and remained a year.[12]

Christmas day was celebrated with a big feast served to the Indians. Mother Amadeus gave each squaw a new dress. Two weeks later they assembled at the mission for another feast. A long procession of 200 Cheyennes came, among them, White Bull, Black Eagle, White Hawk White Frog, Standing Elk, with Leonard Tyler, a Southern Cheyenne, who acted as interpreter.

Mother Amadeus did not return to St. Peter's until August 1898.

*   *   *

1898

Aug. 15 —

On this memorable day, Mother returns to us after an absence of 8 months from Dec. 13, '97 to Aug. 15, '98.

Aug. 16 —

Father A. F. Trivelli, S.J., begins our annual retreat. So far our retreats have been given in the following unbroken chain: 1885—Rev. F. Eberschweiler; 1886—Rev. Jenna; 1887—Rev. P. Tornelli; 1888—Rev. J. Damiani; 1889—Rev. Quinn; 1890—Rev. P. Tornelli; 1891—Rev. Schrorre; 1892—Rev. J. Rebman; 1893—Rev. Neri; 1894—Rev. Neri; 1895— Rev. P. Prando; 1896—Rev. P. Muset; 1897—Rev. d'Asti; 1898—Rev. A.F. Trivelli.

Aug. 24 —

Perl Hendren baptized Ursula.

Aug. 25 —

Perl Hendren makes her First Communion.

Aug. 27 —

Father H. Arts, our Chaplain, returns from his retreat. Miss Rosecrans arrives.

Sept. 2 —

Visit from Rev. J. Vermaat, the very unfriendly pastor at St. Labre's Mission. He was accompanied by Rev. Fr. Gallagher of Kalispell.

Sept. 3 —

The Fathers and Miss Rosecrans left today.

Sept. 10 —

Our dear Mrs. Mannix arrived with Mabel, Mechtilde, Rosella, M. Ursula and Helen.

Sept. 11 —

Mrs. Mannix left today.

Sept. 13 —

Kitty Bradford entered today.

Sept. 16 —

Mrs. Kelly arrived from Benton, leaving here her little Rose.

Sept. 30 —

A herder with a very large band of sheep asked to spend the night in our corral.

Oct. 2 —

Mother M. Rose appointed to go East and watch over our two Novices there.

Oct. 3 —

Winnie and Mary Coleman reached here today from Miles City.

Oct. 9 —

Arrival of Mr. C.S. Haire, architect, to treat with Mother about finishing the house. Mr. Weber, plumber, arrives to see to condition of plumbing before winter.

Oct. 10 —

Mary Fields arrived to pay us a visit. Mr. C.L. Haire returns to Helena.

Oct. 11 —

The threshing machine arrives, thirty-three hands sat down to dinner and supper, and by night we had 1,586 bu. oats stored in our old

151

log cabins. Poor Mary Fields was thrown out of her wagon by a wild horse and reached the mission in sorry plight.

Oct. 12 —

Mary Connelly enters!

Mary Connelly Sullivan, student in the 90's.

153

Oct. 13 —

Threshing machine broken down but the men stayed, chopped wood and got in the garden stuff for their board. Mary Fields spent the night and received Holy Communion this morning. Father Snells sang the High Mass.

Oct. 16 —

Superintendent Campbell of Fort Shaw with his wife and children pay a friendly visit and was entertained with music.

Oct. 17 —

Mother Perpetua returned today bringing our sick little Sister Watzinitha.

Oct. 21 —

Father Sandavet's carpet beautifies our chapel.

Oct. 25 —

Sister Mary Rose left today with Ursula Hendren for a year's study in Philadelphia. Mother left for Great Falls.

Oct. 27 —

Mother at the Falls.

Oct. 31 —

Joyous Hallowe'en ducking for the apples Mother sent from the Falls.

Nov. 4 —

Fire broke out in washhouse but was quelled in time.

Dec. 4 —

A bell weighing 860 lbs., a gift of our dear Father Sandavet, reached Cascade.

1899

Jan. 1 —

The New Year is ushered in by the ringing of Father Sandavet's beautiful bell.

Jan. 13 —

Nora Sullivan returned from Benton.

Jan. 15 —

Fifteen years ago today Mother and her companions left Toledo for Montana.

154

Jan. 25 —

> T. Brown and V. Laroch were married by Rev. H. Arts in the Mission Church. Mother gave to Mechtilde the cap and the name Sister Mary Mechtilde. Sister Mary Mechtilde is the third of the Nascent order of Indian Maidens, "Virgins of the Sacred Heart."

Feb. 11 —

> Sister Mary Mechtilde, who has worn the cap in the new Order just two weeks, died peacefully at 3 o'clock this A.M.

Feb. 12 —

> Frightful wind and snowstorm. For the first time in the history of the Mission, the mail could not get in.

Feb. 13 —

> For the first time in the history of our dear Mission we had Exposition of the Blessed Sacrament and the Forty Hours with High Mass at 5 A.M.

March 25 —

> Mother Angela and Sister St. Genevieve go to Cincinnati, Ohio, with permission of our Bishop.

March 26 —

> Began plowing.

June 26 —

> Our Bishop arrived for the Annual Closing and Episcopal Visitation. Rev. H. Arts met him in Cascade and narrowly escaped death, being thrown between wheels and buggy.

June 29 —

> Closing in boarding school.

155

Indian Children

July 3 —

Mother dispatches for immediate return of Sisters Genevieve and Amata.

July 4 —

Supper at Mother's Rock. Fireworks furnished by Rev. Chaplain.

July 13 —

We enjoy unpacking the box from Philadelphia and seeing our Nuns' work in pyrography and wood carving.

July 14 —

Mrs. Moran brought a welcome gift of home-grown strawberries.

July 17 —

Sisters Philippa and Angela off to Helena to take up land.

July 18 —

Picnic at Mr. Moran's—most delightful; we viewed his new house.

July 19 —

Fathers Diomedi and Damiani sail for South America.

July 21 —

Arrival of Father Delhoor.

July 22 —

Retreat.

*   *   *

[1] Claudia married Con Price, well known cattle man and friend of Charles Russell.

[2] Father Andreis was drowned in the Yellowstone.

[3] Thomas Walsh later became Senator and was appointed to the Cabinet as Attorney General by President Franklin D. Roosevelt.

[4] *Annals.* Dec. 4, 1894.

[5] This log cabin was called "The Opera House."

[6] Annals, St. Peter's, 1896.

[7] Sister Lutegarde left a candle burning in the pew. She had used it to light the charcoal for Benediction.

[8] The Lord rules me and I shall want for nothing.

[9] U. Annals, Vol. 4, Dec. 23, 1893 to June 20, 1897.

[10] Annals, St. Labre's, 1897.

[11] Annals, St. Labre's, 1897.

[12] Miles, John. "San Antonian brought Gospel Despite Death Threats." *San Antonian Evening News.* Nov. 9, 1923.

CHAPTER 7

Education

Miss Lavinia Whitfield of Cincinnati, Ohio, was engaged Oct. 19, 1891 to teach the Sisters carving. They, in turn, taught the Indians. When the Superintendent visited the school in May 1892, he was particularly pleased with this work, and said that he had not seen it in any other Indian school which he had visited.

Miss Whitfield remained with the Sisters until July of the following year. She soon married a rancher, John Farrell, who had worked at the Mission and also on the Jesuits' ranch. After a few years, Mrs. Farrell died, leaving three children, which her husband brought to the Mission to be temporarily cared for.

In August 1896, Sister Annunciata went to Helena to take lessons on the banjo and mandolin from Mrs. Guthrie. This talented Nun taught the Indian girls and organized two orchestras, one for the Indian school and one for the academy.

Two novices, Sister Amata Dunne and Sister De Merici Shebel, went to Philadelphia, in 1898, to study at the Drexel Institute and School of Oratory. They were joined in October by Sister Genevieve Schweitzer, and later, by Sister Mary Rose Galvin and Ursula Hendren. While in Philadelphia, the group lived in a house owned by Mother Katharine Drexel. They studied art, music, oratory, carving and science.

Professor Dwyer was hired in 1900 to teach the nuns and the senior classes of the high school. Among the subjects taught were Greek, Latin, and astronomy. Professor Dwyer later became superintendent of schools in Anaconda, where he was well-known as an educator.

159

Madame Vincent, a vocalist in Helena was engaged in Oct. 1901, to teach singing to the Sisters and advanced pupils of the academy. She had two gifted pupils in Helena, who came with her to St Peter's, Miss Janie Jeffries, a sister-in-law of Norman Holter, and Miss Wells who also taught at the Mission.

In April, Miss Gwedolyn Clark arrived from Cincinnati, to give advance instruction in piano, to both Nuns and pupils.

When the fall term opened in 1900, there was a large enrollment. Mother Amadeus tried a new experiment in the education of the Indians. She brought seven Cheyenne girls and eight boys of the same tribe from St. Labré's to St. Peter's. This new life away from their environment, she hoped, might help the children to adjust to future changes. Each year, they were returned to their families for a vacation. The boys were given horses for their own use and the care of each became their responsibility.

In the school for Indian girls, the kindergarten and primary classes began at ten o'clock and dismissed at twelve, resumed at two o'clock and continued until four. Their program consisted of calisthenics, march or drills, color and form, table work, object lessons, motion songs, arithmetic and board work, singing and slate work, sewing and weaving, spelling and geography.

The intermediate grades began at nine o'clock, continued until twelve, resumed at two until dismissal at four-thirty. Their schedule called for calisthenics, practical arithmetic, language lessons, reading and spelling, grammar, singing, mental arithmetic, geography, writing, and knitting.

The grammar grades were taught voice culture and expression, spelling, arithmetic, grammar, geography, history, penmanship, sight singing, art work and sewing. The art work included crayon, water colors, oil and carving. Sewing included cutting, fitting, dressmaking, running the sewing and buttonhole machines. There were as many as fourteen children at machines at one time.[1] All continued work in knitting, embroidery, and crocheting.

Pupils were detailed for baking, laundry duties, and kitchen work on different afternoons during the week and general housework in the mornings before school. Religious instruction was given outside school hours.

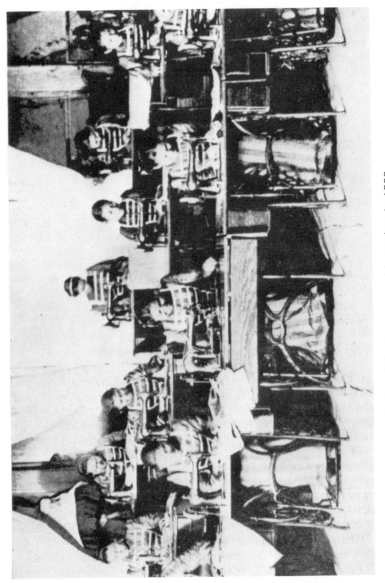

Indian girls at sewing machines taken in 1893.

161

"Crayon work, wood carving, painting in oil and water colors given free of charge to all pupils in grammar department. Instrumental music, piano, and violin free of charge to pupils evincing talent — 30 music pupils in the school this year. Vocal music throughout the school."[2]

Textbooks used included:[3]

McGuffey's *Chart* and *Readers*, One through Six
McGuffey's *Spellers*
Murray's *Grammar*
A. Bearsdell's *Child's Book of Health*
Sadlier's *History of the United States*
Brooks *Arithmetic*
Geography, Electic Series
Shoemaker and Delsarte, *Elocution*

For the upper grades:

Readers by Newell and Creery, and those of Sadlier
Robinson's *Mathematical Series*
Hadley's *English Grammar*
Sadlier's *Geography*, and that of Barnes
J. H. Kellogg, *Physiology* and *Hygiene Charts*

The schedule for the boy's school was somewhat different. The primary classes started at nine o'clock and were dismissed at eleven-thirty. The afternoon session began at two and ended at four-thirty. The program of studies was similar to that of the girls.

From the fourth grade up, the schedule was different. Classes began at nine and continued until noon. In the afternoon, time was devoted to industrial work, except on days of inclement weather when the afternoon sessions began at two and continued until four-thirty.

The primary grades were taught by charts and the other activities were similar to those of the girls.

The intermediate and grammar grades listed: Reading Arithmetic, Letter writing, Penmanship, Grammar, Geography, History, Hygiene and Calisthenics.

The textbooks included:[4]

Sadlier's *First Reader*
The Catholic Publication Society's *First and Second Reader*
Elgar's *Supplementary Primer and Second Reader*
Sadlier's *Geography*
Hadley's *Lessons in Language*
Payson, Dunton and Scribner's *Penmanship*

The enrollment between the years 1885 and 1892 was from an average of 30 to 209. This average continued for the next four years until the Indian boys' school closed in 1896. The enrollment of the Indian girls' school remained at the same level until 1905.

It is interesting to note the various tribes represented by the children. Originally intended as a school for the Blackfeet, it is understandable that the enrollment changed after August 1890 when Holy Family Mission was established on the Two Medicine River for the Blackfeet, Piegans and Blood Indians.

When the St. Peter's Industrial School opened for the girls on March 7, 1885, there were eleven children enrolled, all Blackfeet. In the subsequent years, children from the Assiniboine, Gros Ventre, Soteux, Cree, Iroquois, Snake, Nez Perce, Flathead, Crow and Cheyenne attended the school.[5]

The Cree children were mainly the Métis from Canada, children of the followers of Louis Riel and those who pushed westward from the Red River. There was a large settlement of these people along the Dearborn and around Sullivan Valley and another group in Spring Valley, present Lewistown.

The enrollment of these children caused trouble with the Indian Bureau who complained that pupils listed as Piegan were "with few exceptions" from parents, refugees and followers of Riel. The missionaries asked the department for information as to which were of "Cree half-breed Mothers" and "others" reported as Piegans. The mission authorities claimed they were all American-born.[6]

In the early years, the Piegans and Gros Ventre had the highest enrollment, 105 attending in 1893. During the years 1890, 1891 and 1892, there were 49 Cree girls in the Indian school.[7]

Each child was given religion, music, and art, the core of

163

the curriculum: The child had a precious heritage and tradition in this his right as a child of God and member of the Church. Mother Amadeus put the best works of art on the walls—magnificent copies and prints of the great masters.[8] The children were taught a musical instrument and given lessons in painting and carving. The library with fine selections is still intact.

Supervisor William M. Moss came to visit the school. He was delighted with everything, art work, carving, sewing. The children were dressed for the inspection — the large girls in blue polka dot dresses they had made themselves; the second group, in black and white; and the little ones, in pink. Mr. Moss told the nuns that they had a "very, very good school."

After his visit of inspection, Supervisor Moss wrote the following to the Superintendent of Indian Schools in Washington, D.C.

REPORT OF SUPERVISOR MOSS ON ST. PETER'S MISSION SCHOOL, MONT.

Great Falls, Mont., Aug. 14, 1895.

Hon. Supt. Indian Schools,
Sir:

You have visited the St. Peter's Mission School and know what splendid stone buildings they have. There are practically two schools — the boys' and girls' departments being under distinct and separate management.

The Boys' School:

This department is under the management of the Jesuit Fathers. The sisters at the girls' school do the sewing, washing, breadbaking for them, and they do all the rest of the work. The dormitories are large and commodious — air good. They have a blacksmith-carpenter and shoe shop, but the two former are not open here all the year, and in the latter only mending is done. I consider that practically nothing is done at the trades. The Superintendent says that his observation is that it does not matter so much what the boys work at as that they work, as but a few ever follow their trade after they leave school. The school has a splendid garden and the pupils get first class

164

training in this. They also have a good lot of stock and they are taught to care for it — the most important trade for a Montana boy. They milk 48 cows and have all the milk and butter they can use. Ninety-five pupils were in attendance at the department, not a single one of whom was a *full* blood. The classroom teachers are employed. I enclose the course of study, daily programs, list of textbooks, and from these you can learn all I know about the classroom work. When the weather is not too bad the forenoons are spent in classroom work and the afternoons in industrial. In bad weather school work is the specialty, in good weather, industrial. I find the buildings very clean for bachelor's quarters. The dining room is perhaps a little primitive — no Chinaware but all "granite" and no tablecloths or napkins. Were I to suggest improvements it would be here. I do not see that the boys are any better cared for, or receive any training not given in a reservation school, but few, or none of these are from any reservation, but being gathered up from among settlers — mixed bloods — and it is claimed by outsiders that all are Crees — Canadian Indians who have drifted across the line. It may not be the duty of the U.S. to educate British subjects but these people surely need it as bad as any U.S. Indians. The Fathers claim all are Piegans and it is not impossible that they have Piegan blood as the tribes are only separated by imaginary lines. A pedigree of every child would have to be had to determine.

The Girls' School:

This department is under the management of the Ursuline Sisters, and it is not lacking anywhere. They have three class rooms — one a Kindergarten with 20 to 25 girls from 3 to 6 years old. The K. G. teacher was trained at Normal Institute, Youngstown, Ohio. Most all of the sisters here are from the east and are above the average in education and intelligence. All the girls in the advanced school room are given lessons in instrumental music and oil and crayon painting, wood carving, etc. All are given vocal music.

I am unable to see the necessity of any training or education for a girl, without regard to color, which is not given these girls here. If I were to make any criticism at all, it would be that everything here is so very fine and nice that when they go home the contrast will be too great for them to bear. About 30 white girls attend but they are separate in every way from the Indian girls. There are 15 or 20 full bloods in this department. Course of study, daily programs, and list of textbooks enclosed. Also names of pupils having white father.

Denominational Instruction:

One half hour each day is devoted to denominational instruction in both schools.[9]

Very Respectfully,
Wm. M. Moss, Supr.

[1] Palladino, *Indian and White in the Northwest.* First Ed. Baltimore, 1894, pp. 194, 195, illus.

[2] Course of Study, Daily Program, List of Textbooks for Girls Department, St. Peter's Mission, U.S. Department Indian Affairs, Record Group, 75, 34506. U.S. National Archives, Washington, D.C., 1895.

[3] *Ibid.* (34506), 1895.

[4] *Ibid.*

[5] Reports, St. Peter's Indian Industrial School, 1885-1905.

[6] Letter, Father Andreis to Commissioner of Indian Affairs, March 28, 1892, U.S. National Archives, Washington, D.C., Record Group 75, No. 12446.

[7] Letter, Father Andreis to T.J. Morgan, June 7, 1892, U.S. National Archives Record Group 75, No. 22485.

[8] These pictures are preserved and hang on the walls of the Ursuline Academy. Violins, mandolins, and guitars, cello and harp are kept there as historical treasures.

[9] U.S. National Archives, Record Group 34506, *Indian Office, 1895.*

CHAPTER 8

Friends and Neighbors

Mother Katharine Drexel

Mother Amadeus' greatest benefactor was Mother Katharine Drexel, foundress of the Sisters of the Blessed Sacrament for Indian and colored people.

Katharine was born November 26, 1858, in Philadelphia of Francis Anthony Drexel and Hannah Langstroth Drexel. A few weeks after her birth, her mother died, leaving the infant and her three-year-old sister. An aunt and uncle, the Anthony Drexels, cared for the children in their home until the father's marriage to Emma Bouvier, a deeply religious woman. The third child, Louise, was loved dearly by the two older children who always spoke of her as "the little sister."

Francis Drexel died on February 15, 1885, just two years after his wife. He made a will in which he left one-tenth of his assets to charity, and the remaining $14,000,000, to his three daughters with certain provisions. A trust fund was formed under which the three girls were to have the use of the income. In the event of the death of one, the remaining sisters were to have the use of it. If there were no children on the death of the last survivor, the entire estate was to be divided among the original beneficiaries. Katharine was the last survivor. She lived 96 years, dispensing money to her own schools and those of others to aid the Indian and Negro.

After the death of their father, the three daughters made a trip to Europe and had an interview with Pope Leo XIII. Katharine pleaded with His Holiness for priests for the Indian Missions.

Pope Leo said to her, "Why not, my child, yourself, become a missionary?"

On their return home Father Joseph Stephen, Director of the Bureau of Catholic Indian Missions, persuaded the girls to take a trip west to visit the Indian Missions in the Dakotas. They were accompanied from Omaha by Bishop O'Connor, a longtime friend.

In 1872, Bishop O'Connor, then a young priest, had been named pastor at Holmesburg near Torresdale, the summer home of the Drexels, and he was Katharine's spiritual director. He was appointed Vicar Apostolic of Nebraska in 1876, and his headquarters were in Omaha. It was he who insisted that she found an Order for the explicit work among the Indians and Negroes. She had first wished to enter an Order already established in the church.

For her religious training Katharine went to the novitiate of the Sisters of Mercy at Pittsburgh, and on May 7, 1889, became a postulant. On November 7 she was received as a novice. Because of ill health, Bishop O'Connor was not able to be at the reception ceremony but it is to be noted that Bishop Brondel of Montana was present in the sanctuary. Katharine had already given generously to his missionaries.

During her novitiate the novice experienced great grief. Her dear friend and director, Bishop O'Connor, died on May 27, 1890. Her sister Elizabeth had married Walter George Smith and had gone to Europe on her honeymoon. Shortly after their return to the United States, Elizabeth died. The third sister, Louise, at the time was on the ocean coming back from Europe.

On February 12, 1891, Mother Katharine was professed as the first Sister of the Blessed Sacrament for Indian and Colored People. A site for the future motherhouse had been selected. It was nineteen miles from Philadelphia and was known later as Cornwell Heights. Since the new motherhouse was not ready, it was decided to use the old summer home of the Drexels at Torresdale as a temporary novitiate. By the end of the year there were twenty-eight members in the new community. On February 27, 1885, Miss Katharine Drexel sent a donation of $5000 to Mother Amadeus, and again on December 26 of the same year, $500 more. Another gift of $2000 came on January 17, 1889. A deposit at the Drexel and Company Bank in Philadelphia for $8500 was made in favor of Mother Amadeus. After Mother Katharine's novitiate she began again to contribute, sending $5000 on May 31, 1893.

When the government withdrew its contract, the devoted benefactress again came to the rescue and sent a check for $750, on February 16, 1897, as payment for the board of 30 Indian girls. This was given with the promise of the same quarterly payment in the future with the added condition, "as long as I live."

Mother Katharine kept her promise and until the day the school was burned, November 16, 1918, she never failed to send this needed help.

This tribute was given to Mother Katharine Drexel: "We confess that we view with sadness the fact that one devoted woman gives every year to Indian missions more than all the Catholics of the United States combined.

"Through the munificence of the daughters of Mr. Francis Drexel, school buildings were erected on the reservations for the education of Catholic Indian children at a cost of one million five hundred thousand dollars."[1]

Bishop Brondel was a missionary bishop as he had been a missionary priest. He had the interest of the various tribes at heart and worked for their continued welfare. When he became Bishop of Montana his zeal was constant and he did everything in his power to promote the Indians' cause. When Katharine Drexel received the religious habit, Bishop Brondel was present in Pittsburgh.[2] Later he solicited her aid.

An appeal was sent out from the Bureau of Catholic Indian Missions on January 6, 1903, urging the establishment of the "Society for the Preservation of the Faith among Indian Children," in all dioceses. The Society had been inaugurated in the Diocese of Cleveland in December, 1901. In the appeal was a brief summary of the Indian policy of the United States.

In his message to Congress in 1870, President Grant invited the various religious denominations to cooperate in the work of civilizing and Christianizing the Indians. He realized from the frequent outbreaks and border wars with various Indian tribes that only religion could civilize the Indian and establish peace between him and his white neighbors. He recommended that the various reservations should be divided among the different religious denominations, and, in carrying out this recommendation, the Indian department decided that no minister should be allowed to officiate except on the reservation allotted to his denomination. We will not discuss the justice of this policy. Later on this policy was discontinued. The Indian reservations became a free field of missionary operations for all denominations. The Government promised to assist in a pecuniary way the educational work of all religious societies on the following terms.:

The Government should be liberal in making contracts with religious denominations to teach Indian children in schools established by these denominations. It should throw open the door and say to all denominations, "There should be no monopoly in good works. Enter, all of you, and do whatever your hands may find of good work to do, and in your effort the Government will give to your encouragement out of its liberal purse. . ."

In 1895 it became a law that after five years all appropriations should cease, a twenty per cent reduction being made each year. In 1900, the last payment was made by the Government. Meanwhile, Miss Katharine Drexel had become a Sister and had founded the Community of the Blessed Sacrament for the education of Indians and Negroes. Had it not been for her generous help, the Catholic contract schools would long since have been suspended. She has for many years given liberally to different schools and missions, and, since the withdrawal of Government aid, has contributed about $85,000 annually for maintaining the contract schools. . . .We confess that we view with sadness the fact that one devoted woman gives every year to Indian missions more than all the Catholics in the United States combined.

The appeal was signed by James Cardinal Gibbons of Baltimore, Archbishop Farley of New York, and Archbishop Ryan of Philadelphia.[3]

Mary Fields

171

MARY FIELDS

One of the most loved characters who lives in the memory of the Montana Ursulines was Mary Fields. The oldtimers called her "Black Mary" and they, too, loved and respected her. When Mother Amadeus was near death from pneumonia in April, 1885, Mary came to Montana to help the missionaries.

She was of the Negro race, born in slavery in Tennessee on May 15, 1832. She lived in Mississippi for a time, and then found employment at the Ursuline Convent in Toledo. When Mother Amadeus' brother was left a widower in Florida, Mother sent Mary there to care for his five children, who were then brought to Toledo and sent on to a convent boarding school in Canada.

After Mother Amadeus recovered from pneumonia, Mary remained, intending to spend her life helping with the difficult chores at the Mission. She directed the washing but always did the church and sacristy linens herself. She raised a fine garden, and at one time had 400 chickens.

When Father Lindesmith, the Army chaplain at Fort Keough, visited the Mission in the summer of 1887, he enjoyed Mary's account of an encounter with a skunk. The beast had invaded the chicken coop, killed 62 of the baby chicks, and piled them in a heap. She killed the skunk with a hoe and dragged the carcass a mile to the Convent to show the Sisters.

Moving from the old log cabins to the new stone building was an event. Bishop Brondel supervised the move, but Mary took charge of Mother Amadeus' belongings, wheeling her loads in an old wheelbarrow across the bridge to the new home.

Mary did the freighting for the Mission and sometimes the roads were impassable, that is, to all but Mary. Once a pack of wolves frightened the horses. The load was upset, but she stood guard all night to protect the provisions which she knew could not be replaced. Fighting a blizzard, with no road in sight this indomitable woman walked back and forth through the night to keep from freezing.

One of the Sisters thought it a good idea to take advantage of Mary's absence on a trip and clean out the laundry, as they called it. There was nearly a disaster. The Sisters gathered a pile of trash, fed the fire with it when a sharp report was heard. Sister Gertrude was shot. A bullet in the trash went off and hit her over the eye.

There were years of happy living for Mary, who had no fear of man or beast and could lick two men, it was said.

One day Mother Angela and Sister Elizabeth Amrhein, a postulant, were leaving to start a new Mission at Arlee on the Jocko Reservation. Father Ebershweiler, S.J., had been visiting at the Mission and was traveling as far as Cascade with them. One of the horses broke loose and cracked a singletree. Mary was at the scene and trouble arose between her and the ranch foreman, Mr. Burns, over a new and old harness. Mr. Burns, so the story goes, "made a grimace at Mary. This aroused her ire; she hit him with a stone the size of a man's fist. Luckily, Father Andreis put a timely end to the untimely quarrel by telling Mr. Burns to go back to his work."

Not long after this, Mary and Mr. Mosney touched rifles, but there was no firing.

The Sisters provided for all of Mary's wants — board, clothing, spending money, cartridges, and tobacco. Some unkind soul even complained to the Bishop about her. She was at times troublesome, but her unfailing loyalty endeared her to the Nuns and children.

Unexpectedly, word came from the Bishop to send Mary Fields away. It came as a blow to all. Mary was part of their mission, and it was understood that she would live there and be cared for as long as she lived. Mary was indignant and declared she would go to the Bishop and "make him bring witnesses to swear to what they said about her." There is no record of the interview.

Mother arranged for her to live in Cascade and was helpful in obtaining the mail route for her. Mary drove the mail coach triumphantly into St. Peter's, never missing a trip. Later, she had a little cottage in Cascade where she took in washing and had an eating house.

After leaving the Mission Mary was not always faithful to her religious obligations. On one trip the horses became unmanageable and Mary was badly injured. She became repentant and the Nuns used the occasion to encourage her to return to her religious duties. The next morning at Mass she appeared, not as the prodigal in the back of the chapel, but in the front pew, resplendent in a blue challis dress and her usual long white veil for chapel. One of the Sisters had labored far into the night to make this lovely dress for Mary's return to God.

The little town of Cascade is situated about fifteen miles from St. Peter's. It came into existence with the Montana Central railroad, built by Broadwater to connect Helena with the Great Northern which reached Great Falls in 1887. It was the home for a time of Charlie Russell, the cowboy artist. In a pen and ink sketch, "A Quiet Day in Cascade," Russell immortalized Mary. He depicts her as being upset by a kicking mule which causes her basket of eggs to fall. The artist very cleverly wove into that picture several important events in the history of the town.

Mary died in Columbus Hospital in Great Falls in 1914, and was buried in the little cemetery beneath the ridge on the road to her loved Mission.[4]

THOMAS MORAN

One of the oldest and best friends of the Mission, Thomas Moran, had charge of the Mission property during the years 1866 - 1874, when the Jesuit Fathers only visited there occasionally.

This loyal friend was born in Ireland, and his birthday, or rather, baptismal day, March 4, was always observed. The Sisters made a decorated cake for each anniversary. From Ireland he came to Massachusetts, then went West by way of Panama to California and Oregon, thence to Last Chance Gulch. There he worked with Thomas Cruse and Robert Thoroughman. Moran was a member of a party which came in the Sun River stampede following a false rumor of the discovery of gold there.

Thomas Moran settled on a claim in the valley just two miles from St. Peter's, at a beautiful spot near the mountains and next to Mr. Ed Lewis' claim. He was married by Father Imoda on November 25, 1880, to Mary Ann Heany, a cousin to Mrs. John D. Brown. The Moran children all attended the Academy at the Mission.[5]

ED LEWIS

Ed Lewis was born Mary 18, 1837, in Cambria Country, Pennsylvania. The family moved to Iowa and there he worked on his father's farm and received his early education. In 1854, he began work on a steamboat on the Mississippi and Missouri Rivers.

When he was eighteen, Lewis was hired by the American Fur Company to go to Fort Benton. He left St. Louis on the *Star of the West*, which went as far as Fort Union, and then traveled to Fort Benton in a mackinaw boat. For some years he worked between Fort Benton and Fort Union, carrying goods for the fur trade. He had many adventures. On one he was sent from Fort Benton to Hell Gate River by Major Boaks with a message to Captain Mullen. Traveling with Mr. Dawson, the pair had a narrow escape when harassed by Crow Indians between Benton and Fort Union.

In 1864 Lewis went to the mines at Mitchell and Silver City. The next year, together with Malcolm Clark, he obtained a charter to build a toll wagon road through Prickly Pear Canyon.

He worked in the Sun River valley in '68 and spent that winter in the abandoned St. Peter's Mission on the Missouri near the present town of Ulm.

In the spring of 1869 he took up a claim not far from the new site of St. Peter's. His ranch and that of Tom Moran adjoined, but his lay at the foot of the mountains, although their homes were only a few hundred feet apart.

That same year Lewis married the daughter of Meek-i-appay or Heavy Shield, a Piegan. The couple had three children, Isabell, Theresa, and Mollie, brought up in the loving atmosphere of a Christian home. Mollie was one of the original group to attend the opening of St. Peter's in 1884.[6]

ISABELL TABOR

Mrs. Tabor was born in Silver City on May 11, 1866, the daughter of Edward Lewis, one of Montana's pioneers and early settlers in the Mission valley. Coming to Montana in May, 1857, he was employed by the American Fur Company

175

for some years. In 1863 he began prospecting at Silver City where Isabell was born. Five years later Lewis settled in the Mission Valley and remained there until his death in 1914.

Isabell's mother was Sycowwastakapi, the daughter of a Piegan chief, Meekiappy, known also as Cut Hand. Her grand-aunt, Black Bear, was the mother of Mrs. Malcolm Clark. When Isabell was born, Black Bear told her mother that she would see to it that this child would have a long life; she would sacrifice part of her to the Great Spirit. Her mother's children had died in infancy and early childhood, so in order to insure the longer life of the infant, Black Bear cut off the first joint of the little finger on her right hand and buried it. "Black Bear offered part of me to the Great Spirit, buried it in the ground and prayed that I might live to be very old," related Mrs. Tabor, and added, "I had several brothers and sisters, but I am the only one living."

Her early childhood was impressed by the missionaries, laboring and struggling at the Mission. She loved to tell of the days when the family walked from their ranch home by way of Saddle Back Mountain to attend Mass in the little cabin of Father Imoda. When the missionaries moved St. Peter's from its earlier location on the Missouri to its present site, they built three cabins close to the little canyon and farther removed from the present road that now winds through the valley. Isabell Tabor remembered the crude altar with an oilcloth canopy necessary to keep the dirt roof from sifting through on the altar. She could point out the exact spot where these cabins stood. Now only a few stones mark the spot.

She remembered Brother Claessens who came to Montana with the first group of Jesuits in 1840, and who labored in his later years at St. Peter's. She recalled how Brother John carved the altar which now stands in the old church. Among her treasured possessions was a crucifix given her mother by Father Rappagliosi who died in 1878 while on a mission attending to the spiritual care of the Indians along the Milk River. She loved the handmade rosary that Father Prando made and gave to her. Indeed there is scarcely one among the early missionaries whom she did not see or know at the Mission.

During her school years there was only the boys' school at

St. Peter's. The Ursulines did not open the girls' school until 1884, so Isabell was sent to St. Vincent's Academy in Helena from 1878 to 1881. She traveled there on the old stagecoach along the Mullan Road, taking a day and a night for the trip. When she left for school in the fall of 1878, the little church was just built and was in use when she returned the following summer.

Isabell Lewis was married on July 12, 1881 to John Tabor who was foreman on the Mission ranch operated by the Jesuits. In 1863 the couple moved to their own ranch above the Mission where Mrs. Tabor lived until shortly before her death. She was the mother of five children, two of whom, John Leo and Mary Margaret, are still living, and she was very proud of her fourteen grandchildren and twenty great-grandchildren.[7]

SAM FORD

Sam Ford was born near Montreal, Canada, on June 29, 1833. He went West to St. Paul, Minnesota, and then to St. Louis, when he was only nineteen years of age. At St. Louis he stowed away on the steamer, *Chippewa*, headed for the Upper Missouri. Just above Fort Union the boilers exploded. When the passengers and crew were assembled on the river bank, the Captain took roll call. He discovered that he had one extra passenger, Sam Ford! For a time Ford worked at Fort Benton, then in Sun River valley, prospected, and finally started a cattle ranch of 7000 acres near Augusta.

In 1872 he married Miss Clement La Pier. Their children, Louisa, Millie or May, and Josephine, all attended the Academy and little Eddie the boys' school.

Joe Ford, a son, married Anna Keough in the Mission church. The family came from Augusta the day before, stayed overnight, and were entertained at a wedding breakfast in the Convent. Anna Keough was the little girl of six years who, with Maggie Fox, were at the home of Mrs. Armstrong on the Teton when she was murdered in June, 1881. Later, Anna lived with the T. H. Clewells in Helena.

Sorrow came to the family when their little Eddie died. He was in the boys' school when he became ill. His father came from Augusta and Doctor Sweat from Great Falls.

Eddie died on January 31, 1896, and was buried from the Mission church.[8]

THOMAS E. BRADY

Thomas E. Brady was born in St. Antoine parish in Quebec on July 31, 1857. He was of Irish descent both on his father's and his mother's side. After his education in Canada, he began the study of law in Plattsburg, New York. From there he came to Helena in 1886 but remained only a few months. On May 16, 1887, the new lawyer arrived in Great Falls and began his practice. He had been married in Plattsburg to Miss Marceline Chauvin, and the couple had three children, all born in Great Falls.

Later, Mr. and Mrs. Chauvin came from Plattsburg to live with the Bradys, and brought along their horses. The family carriage was always drawn by a fine team, and the children in their pony cart were a familiar sight on the streets.

Mr. Brady occupied law offices in the Phelps Block on Central Avenue in the 400 block. Most of the legal business of the Sisters was taken care of by "Lawyer Brady," *gratis*. He and his wife made frequent trips to St. Peter's for the school and convent events.[9]

JOHN D. BROWN

John D. Brown was one of the good neighbors and longtime friends of Mother Amadeus and the Sisters at the Mission. In 1867 his ranch was located at the edge of Shaw Butte, where he had a small trading post. To all the oldtimers, he was known as "Whiskey" Brown, not because of his fondness for that beverage but because he dispensed the much-desired commodity in that locale.

Brown had left St. Paul, Minnesota, for the West in 1858 and, after almost incredible hardships, came to Fort Benton in '59. In the spring of 1860 he hired out to Captain Mullan to help build bridges on the Mullan Road in the Washington Territory. When he arrived in Walla Walla on October, 1860, Brown soon left Mullan and went to The Dalles in Oregon. He worked in the vicinity of the Columbia River cutting timber for a navigation company, then went to Gold Creek and on to Bannock. There he heard of the gold findings in Prickly Pear Valley near Montana Bar. In January of 1863, he was in Fort Benton where he took up with a man named Thibeau and with whom he returned to the Prickly Pear. Brown's friend, Bill Sweeney, had a claim at Alder Gulch and sent for him but when he reached the Gulch someone had jumped the claim.

Brown then went back to Montana Bar near present Helena, and there met with a crippling accident. A falling log rolled upon him, pinning his leg against the stump. He was able to get free but the leg was broken and there was no chance of reaching a doctor, so the cripple spent the winter in a little cabin with a man he hired to cook for him.

Knowing Father Ravalli's fame as a surgeon and that the priest was stationed at St. Peter's, Brown was determined to reach him. He gave all his interest in a mine to a man named Merrill to take him to Malcolm Clark's place at the head of Prickly Pear Canyon. There he paid Mr. Morgan $250, every cent he had, to get him the rest of the way, fifty miles to the Mission. When he finally arrived, Father Ravalli was away, but Father Giorda offered to care for him. Father operated on the leg and by the summer of 1865 the former invalid was able to work.[10]

The two Brown girls, Mollie and Annie, were among the first three pupils to enroll at the Mission school on November 10, 1884. Their sister, Theresa, entered later. From the very beginning, Mr. Brown's charity to the Sisters was continuous. He gave the first donation of $100 to Mother Amadeus when she arrived there in 1884.[11]

FATHER J. J. DOLS

Father Dols had often come to the Mission during the summer holidays. He was a great pioneer and an indefatigable worker. He was born in Sittara, Holland, on March 6, 1848. As a youth he studied for the priesthood at the University of Louvain and was ordained in Brussels in 1874, for the Archdiocese of Oregon. His first assignment was to McMinnville, Oregon, where he built the first church there. For a time he was stationed at Gervais and in 1881 was sent to Montana. As the first resident pastor in Butte, he built St.

179

Patrick's Church which was dedicated in September, 1884. Father Dols was instrumental in obtaining the Sisters of Charity of Leavenworth for St. James Hospital there. He took a trip back to his native land in December, 1885. On his return the next year he went to Laurin. Assigned to Dillon, he built a church and rectory there in 1887.

Father Dols was transferred to Great Falls in February, 1891, where he became the first pastor. The church, St. Ann's, had been built by Father A.H. Lambaere and had been dedicated on Rosary Sunday, 1890. The new pastor built the rectory with his own money and willed it to the Church. His territory extended over the entire area of Cascade County, and he zealously cared for this extensive parish. This selfless pastor and missionary died May 30, 1898, at Columbus Hospital in Great Falls and is buried in old Mount Olivet cemetery.[12]

DR. FRANCIS JOSEPH ADAMS

Doctor Francis Joseph Adams was born in Fort Cook, California, on December 16, 1859. His father, John Adams, was a military man who had taken part in the Mexican War and later fought in the Civil War. His mother, Georgina McDougall, was the daughter of Brigadier General Charles McDougall.

Dr. Adams attended Washington University in St. Louis and Georgetown in Washington, D.C. As a surgeon in the regular army, the doctor was first stationed at Fort Hamilton, Long Island, and then at Fort Adams, Newport, Rhode Island. In 1883 he was sent to Montana and assigned to Fort Assiniboine until 1887, then he became an assistant instructor at St. Louis University. Returning to Montana in 1889, he lived at Fort Benton. In 1890 Dr. Adams married Miss Alice Conrad, daughter of Colonel J.W. Conrad of Virginia. The couple moved to Great Falls, where the doctor established himself as a surgeon and general practitioner. Interested in medical facilities for the city, he built the first hospital which was later taken over by the Sisters of Providence. After they erected Columbus Hospital, the doctor organized a school for nurses in 1896.

Dr. Adams was a devoted friend of St. Peter's Mission. It

was never too inconvenient or difficult for him to make the trip to the Mission when he was needed. With his wife he often was a guest at the closing exercises of the school and at the reception and profession ceremonies of the Sisters. At one time he brought his mother who was visiting him.[13]

LOUIS RIEL

Louis Riel's mother, Julie, was the daughter of the first white woman to live in the Canadian Northwest. Marie Ann Gaboury of Three Rivers married Jean Baptiste Lajimodiere, a fur trader, with whom she went west to the Red River country. Her daughter, Julie, married Louis Riel, a Métis, who led in their attempt to gain recognition of their rights in the newly-formed province of Manitoba, and later, in Saskatchewan.

Their son, Louis, was born at St. Boniface in 1844, and because of his intelligence and piety, Archbishop Tache encouraged him to attend the Sulpician College in Montreal to study for the priesthood. After ten years Louis returned to Red River without completing his studies. At the seminary he had been considered "brilliant, but a bit odd." He had a deep and sincere faith, but was taciturn and at times aloof.

After working some months in St. Paul, he went home to his mother at St. Vital on the Assiniboine.

There was unrest in Rupert's Land of the Northwest. Negotiations had been made to transfer its control from the Hudson Bay Company to Canada. The Métis objected. . . .There was also a movement of the Fenians, a group of Irish patriots, to prevent the land from coming under Canadian control. Then a group of American settlers on the south border of Canada and others living along the Red River to the north advocated transfer to the United States.

A governor-designate who attempted to establish his authority in that region was prohibited from entering the territory. The Métis, under the leadership of Louis Riel, formed a resistance movement, resistance to establishment of a government in their territory without their consent or insurance that their land and civil rights would be protected.

They felt justified since the only authority in that region

181

of the Northwest was the Hudson Bay Company, and it had signed away its authority. There had been no proclamation from the Queen as yet, so the Métis felt free to act.

A provisional government was set up for the new province of Manitoba, which means "place of God," or, "The God that speaks." The government pledged its loyalty to Canada, and was promised its "Bill of Rights." Amnesty was also promised for all those who had taken part in the resistance. Louis was banished for five years because of his part in the resistance.

After spending some time in the eastern United States, Louis Riel came back to the Red River country. However, he found it would be difficult to live there; many of his people left for new frontiers. Still hoping that he could do something for his people, he moved on to Montana where there were several settlements of Métis—Milk River and at Spring Valley or Lewistown, and along the Dearborn in the vicinity of St. Peter's Mission. He stayed for a time at Carrol a small point on the Missouri, which had come into existence through river traffic. When the river was too low to allow steamers to go on up to Fort Benton, freight was unloaded at this point. Since it was situated at the beginning of the "Bad Lands" or "breaks" along the river, in Louis' time it was a hangout for outlaws and rustlers. Here Riel was interpreter between the Metis and whites. In April, 1881, he married Marguerite Monette, daughter of Jean Monette. A son was born to the couple whom they called Jean.

Two years later, Riel was offered a position as teacher in the boys' school at St. Peter's. There he lived with the James Swan family in a small cabin where his second child, Marie Angelique, was born. This was the year of the intense cold, but the family managed to survive.

During Mass on June 4, 1884, Louis was called outside to speak to four visitors who had come from Saskatchewan—Gabriel Dumont, Moiese Ouelette, and Michael Dumac, all Métis, and an English half-breed, James Isbister. These men had come to ask Riel to head a movement of protest in an effort to right their grievances against Canada.

Louis Riel accepted and left on June 10 with his wife and family, heading first for Fort Benton. There Father

Eberschweiler tried to dissuade him from the cause. As he left, Riel called out to Father, "I see a gallows on the top of that hill, and I am swinging from it." It was a prophetic farewell.

Louis Riel went to Batoche, a small Métis settlement on the Saskatchewan River. From there he launced his mission, his campaign for justice for his people, both economic and political redress. The appeal declared that the people of the Northwest were not happy under Canadian rule; they were denied the "enjoyment of the right of people." For some time, they had been appealing for "security on their lands, land grants or subsidies for schools, and their patience was running out."

When the government sent police reinforcements into the region it was a signal to the Métis to resist. Led by Gabriel Dumont they overcame the government troops at Duck Lake. Later at Batoche, the Métis were outnumbered and forced to surrender. Dumont escaped across the border to Montana, but Louis gave himself up to the government. He was tried and found guilty of treason and sentenced to be hanged. The sentence was carried out November 16, 1885. With Riel died the hopes and longings of the Métis for a land they could call their own.[14]

RALPH DECAMP

Ralph DeCamp, the Helena artist, was a frequent visitor at St. Peter's. His wife, the former Margaret Hilger, was a talented violinist and frequently spent holidays and vacation time teaching the Sisters and advanced pupils there. After the birth of the son, Renan, in 1897 his mother brought him with her. One of the Sisters described him as that "little terror."

Ralph DeCamp was born in Attica, New York. His family moved to Wisconsin near Milwaukee. Ralph studied under F.A. Lyndston, a well known Milwaukee artist. The family moved to Moorhead, Minnesota, in 1871, but Ralph went to high school in Duluth. When he finished there he studied art in Philadelphia.

With the help of Charles Fee of the Northern Pacific he went to Yellowstone Park with a friend, L.L. Ferron, in

1885. Here he took pictures and painted. In 1886, he stopped in Helena and decided to remain there.

DeCamp had married in 1878 but his wife died shortly after, leaving a son Eddie, aged fifteen months. In 1890 the artist married Margaret Hilger, daughter of Judge Nicholas Hilger, and sister of David Hilger. They had one son, Renan, who became a talented pianist and also an electrical genius. After graduating from Montana State University he worked for the Montana Power Company and then went to Pittsburgh to Westinghouse. He married a Helena girl, Louise Waterbury. They had a son, Renan, also a musician, who lives with his mother in Cranford, New Jersey.

DeCamp painted a panoramic view of St. Peter's Mission, one of his finest works. The mission nestles near the background of Mount Ursula and Fishback. It encompasses a complete view from the "Opera House" on the right to the little log church on the left. Two Ursulines are in the foreground surveying the whole.

The peaceful valley shows the field with its old-time mows of hay in orderly rows. The large stone building of the girls' school has a prominent place, and across the road is the Jesuit house and boys' school.

EDDIE CURRY

The region around St. Paul's Mission in the Little Rockies was the home of one of the most elusive groups of bandits that the West ever produced. That was the Currys, Harvey or Kid, Loney and John Curry. Loney was married to Elfie, the daughter of Pike Landusky, whom Kid Curry had killed because of his mistreatment when Pike was sheriff.

On April 24, 1899, little Eddie Curry, the son of Loney, was enrolled in the boys' school at St. Peter's. The board, washing and tuition at the time was $10 per month. On March 10, 1900, Mother received a payment of a $100 bill on the Curry account.[15] When the money was sent to the bank in Helena, Mother received a letter promptly from the president asking where she got a certain bank note. It was part of the loot from the Wilcox train robbery on the Union Pacific.

At 4:00 A.M. on June 2, 1899, the Northern Pacific No. 1

Express was held up by six armed men in the pouring rain, half a mile from Wilcox Station in Wyoming. The safe was blown open and its contents carried off. Engineer Jones was severely injured in the explosion. A bridge in front of the train was dynamited and another, two miles away, was fired to prevent the second section of the train from coming up.[16]

Loney Curry was finally shot by Pinkerton detectives at Dodson, Missouri, while at the home of his aunt, the mother of Bob Lee, alias Bob Curry.[17]

Little Edward remained at St. Peter's until February 1, 1900. Payments were made on this account until the last cent was paid.

[1] *Letter*, Bureau of Catholic Indian Missions to the Bishops of the U.S., Jan. 6, 1903.

[2] Sr. Consuela Maria Duffy, *Katharine Drexel*, p. 151.

[3] *Letter to the Bishops from the Catholic Indian Bureau*, Ursuline Annals, vol. 5, p. 133.

[4] *Ursuline Annals*, St. Peter's, vol. 3, p. 20.

[5] *Great Falls Yesterdays*, p. 248.

[6] *Progressive Men of Montana*, pp. 1610, 1611. Vaughn, *Then and Now*, pp. 130-140.

[7] Interview with Isabell Tabor in 1944. Article written by author for *Rocky Mountain*, 1944.

[8] Lucille Brady Kranz, Interview. See also: *Progressive Men of Montana*, pp. 528, 529.

[9] *Ibid.*, 560-561.

[10] Vaughn, *Then and Now*,

[11] *Ursuline Accounts*

[12] *Progressive Men of Montana*, pp. 3,4.

[13] *Ursuline Annals.*

[14] Howard, *Strange Empire*, pp. 318-362.

[15] *Accounts*, St. Peter's.

[16] *The Daily Intermountain*, Butte, Friday P.M., June 2, 1899.

[17] Charles A. Sirango, *Riata and Spurs* (Cambridge: Riverside Press, 1927) pp. 208-222.

CHAPTER 9

The End of an Era

On July 29, 1899, Cardinal Vanutelli, Prefect of the Sacred Congregation, sent a letter to all Bishops who had Ursulines in their dioceses. He pointed out that it frequently happened that some had difficulties in carrying out their work for lack of means.

"To obviate these difficulties and disadvantages this Congregation of Bishops and Regulars thought good to grant the request of some Bishops who desired last year that a certain union might be formed between Convents of Ursulines and by a Decree of the 8th of October, 1898, it enacted that if any of these convents in any part of the world wished to be united, their wish would meet with favorable response. Now several convents of Ursulines have written to us quite recently from different countries, asking that the whole Order might form a single body."[1]

The Ursuline Convents of Blois in France and those of Rome and Calvi in Italy had already formed a union to enable them to exchange subjects. Union would be a great advantage for Convents in countries whose laws were passed restricting the teaching apostolate, to be able to send Sisters to other countries.

On Thursday, October 25, 1900, Mother Amadeus left St. Peter's for Rome with Marie Stuart Kolinzuten. At Cascade they met Mother Angela that afternoon, and the following morning left for Chicago by the Great Northern and Baltimore and Ohio Railroad to visit Washington, Philadelphia and New York. They sailed from the latter on November 1 on the *Aquitaine* for LeHavre, en route to the big meeting in Rome for the Roman Union of Ursulines. Arriving at LeHavre, Thursday night, November 9, the trio

187

traveled across France and Italy, reaching Rome on November 13.

The first exercise of the Ursulines opened on November 15 in the evening with Benediction of the Blessed Sacrament and a fine discourse by Father Lenius. On November 16, Cardinal Satolli said Mass and opened the first General Chapter of the Ursulines.

Later Mother wrote, "The Union of the Ursulines is consummated. This evening (November 21) sixty-three (63) houses representing 1900 Ursulines went solid for the Union."

On December 10, Mother continued:

O, such a time as I have had for the last four weeks. No words of mine can describe it—I have been sick, sick for over three weeks in bed, under the doctor's care for several days. The trouble was nothing but pleurisy, but I suffered much here without a fire in a very cold, damp room on the north side of the house. Now I have a room facing east and I am getting along better, but my hands are so frozen. I have not seen a fire since I left our own dear hearth—oh, I wish I had a stick of wood for a Christmas present.

Very Reverend Mother St. Julian was elected Prioress General;

Mother St. Ignatius of Frankfort-on-the-Main, First Assistant General;

Mother Angela of Montana, Second Assistant (Imagine my difficulties for Anaconda and Miles City);

Mother St. Stanislaus of Aix, France, Third Assistant;

Mother Maria Pia of Saluzzo, Fourth Assistant;

Mother Blessed Sacrament of Bazas, France, Treasurer General;

Mother Stanislaus of Aix is also Secretary General.

We demanded an American representative in the seat of Government, Rome, on the principle of American Independence, "no taxation without representation." I was proposed for the representative but I told them I could not accept, as I was pledged to a very special work from which I could not be spared for at least a year. So I think I am free. Thank God and Mary.

Mother wrote that she expected to leave Rome on December 16 to visit Calvi at the request of Reverend Mother General. "The thought of home makes me happy. I hope when I get home I shall never be cross again. There is but little change in our dress. The Chapter adopted our headdress with a slight change in our guimpe—habit like San Antonio, Crucifix like Brown County, ring, train, skirt in place of mantle, long veil, our leather girdle is kept (D.G.) and black cottes in place of grey. The Union is projected on a very broad basis, there is no cause for alarm, you will all be satisfied, I hope."[2]

From Calvi, Mother Amadeus went to Assisi, Foligno, and to the shrine of Santa Clara near Foligno, then to Loretto. She arrived in New York on February 26, 1901, having been sick throughout the voyage, and had to go to St. Vincent's Hospital. Later, she traveled to Cornwell Heights in Pennsylvania to see her dear friend, Mother Katharine Drexel. She then stopped at Pittsburgh and was at Toledo, Ohio, on March 30.

The traveler finally arrived home at St. Peter's on April 24. The bell rang out with a joyful welcome, for as one nun wrote, "A welcome from Rome is a thing of a lifetime."[3]

The following year began with bitter cold weather—so cold that the boarders who had gone home for vacation were unable to return. Temperatures went down to 37° below zero and snow drifts were 14 feet high. Pipes broke and flooded rooms, causing the ceiling to fall in one of the classrooms. Coal was ordered from Lethbridge and delivered at Cascade at $5.00 a ton.[4]

Father Arts, the pastor and chaplain, was replaced by Father Malo on March 19. Plans were made for a new church to replace the original log structure and ground was broken by Tom Moran and Ed Lewis. When Bishop Brondel came for the closing exercises, he laid the cornerstone on June 30.

The preceding day, thirty-five were confirmed and the closing exercises were held for the Academy and Indian

Schools. Three postulants were received, among them Sister Camilla Fouts of Spokane, a saintly religious dear to everyone who ever knew her.

In the fall, Father Malo was replaced by Father Prudenz, described as "a little boyish-looking priest of only twenty-seven summers."

Sister Mary Rose and Sister Amata with little Kokomekis (Elsie Gardipee) went to St. Paul, Toledo and Cleveland. Little Kokomekis, whose name meant "moon," was dressed in a beautifully beaded buckskin outfit. Sister Amata returned to St. Paul from Toledo where she remained to study portrait painting. At this time Miss Gwendolyn Clark of Cincinnati was hired to teach piano to the Sisters and advanced pupils.

It was on May 31 that the Ursulines at St. Paul's Mission moved into their new stone convent and school from the old log buildings they had inhabited since 1887. The new building was built by the charity of Mother Katharine Drexel.

On June 29 there was an outstanding program by the older students and the graduates of the academy. The convent orchestra, consisting of violins, mandolins, guitars, harp and piano performed. Those taking part were Mabel Mannix, Honora Coleman, Margaret Moran, Mary Hollenbach, Edna White, Katherine Norton, Mabel O'Connell, Ursula Moran, Jane Jeffries, Nora Sullivan, Mary Coleman, Rose Hollenbach, Pearl White, Mary Lorena Dawson, Mary Sullivan, Anna Seilnacht, Valine Fisher, Mary Slominsky, and Louise Kelly.

The theme, "The Mystic Lessons of the Grail Legends," was portrayed in prose and poetry. Margaret Moran gave the Salutatory and Winifred Coleman, the Valedictory.

There was a four-piano piece, a selection from Czerny, played by Misses Gwendolyn Clark, Margaret Moran, Mabel Mannix, and Winifred Coleman.

Sixteen young ladies performed a thirty-two hand piece, the Overture, "Semiramide," of Rossini, concerted by Czerny. It was an impressive exhibition in this out of the way spot in the wilderness. The Misses Louise Kelly, Lorena Dawson, Pearl White, Gwendolyn Clark, Mabel Manix, Margaret Moran, Winifred Coleman, Jane Jeffries, Mary Hollenbach, Anna Seilnacht, Nora Sullivan, Mary Coleman,

Moran, Winifred Coleman, Katherine Norton, Ursula Moran, Valine Fisher, and Mary Slominsky.

The seven graduates who received high school diplomas were Winifred Coleman, Margaret Moran, Mabel Mannix, Pearl White, Mary Hollenbach, Lorena Dawson and Mabel O'Connell.

This first graduation at St. Peter's took place on June 29, 1902, in the "Opera House" decorated for the occasion. Exercises for the different departments took more than one day.

Bishop Brondel arrived on June 27 and the programs started the following day. The boys, St. Joseph's Academy, gave theirs at 10:30 A.M. It was the first time that they had performed by themselves. Some were talented, especially Harvey and Grant Smith who played the violin and piano.

In the afternoon the girls of the academy held their recital, music numbers and recitations.

In the evening of that day the Indian girls' program was given. It began with a selection by the Minnehaha Club composed of twenty-eight girls playing violins, mandolins, and guitars. Anna Pukanaki made an address to the Bishop in her native tongue. The group then presented a play, "Elmona," during which seven Cheyenne girls gave a dance.

All the girls of the Academy left the next day for Anaconda where they gave an entertainment at the Margaret Theatre.

Fire destroyed the convent at Miles City, November 28, 1897, as the result of an overheated stove. The school was temporarily closed and the Nuns returned to St. Peter's.

Furniture that had been saved was stored in Miles City, but in September of 1900 word was received that the building which housed it had been burned.

Miles City was the first Ursuline foundation in Montana and was very dear to the Ursulines. On Bishop Brondel's request that the Nuns return there "for the sake of the Church in Eastern Montana," Mother Amadeus engaged an architect, Mr. O'Haire, to draw up plans and construct a new convent. It was built on a more suitable site at Leighton Boulevard, and was of red brick, Colonial style, with white pillars in front. The inside finish and stairways and the deep wainscoting in the halls were of solid oak.

Left to right: Lorena Dawson, Pearl White, Margaret Moran, Winifred Coleman, Mabel Manix, Mary Hollenbach, Mabel O'Connell.

Graduates — 1902

192

The building was finished in the fall of 1902. Mother Amadeus left St. Peter's on October 3 with Mothers Caecilia, Lutegarde, Amata, and two Cheyenne girls to open the new school. A few miles from Billings the train was wrecked, and Mother Amadeus was severely injured. She was taken to St. Vincent's Hospital in Billings where the injury was diagnosed as an impacted fracture of the femur. On November 4 she was moved to Helena so that she could be under the care of Dr. Treacy. There her friends were extremely kind, showering on her every attention. She especially enjoyed a group who called on her after the wedding of Charles Benton Power, son of T. C. Power, to Miss Mabel Larson. Governor and Mrs. Toole, Major and Mrs. McGinnis, the Misses Nannie and Florence Fortune, all came in evening dress. When Mother was able to be about, Mrs. Thomas Carter and Mrs. Treacy often took her for rides.

Dr. Treacy advised sending her to California where the climate was mild and she could recuperate more easily. Mother left Helena with Sister Caecilia on April 3, 1903, for San Diego. The pair rented a little cottage at Coronado. Mother Angela Lincoln arrived in Cincinnati from Rome in April, and then went on to California. Mother Caecilia returned to Montana and Miles City. In July Mother Amadeus went to Los Angeles for necessary treatment. She suffered from a stiff knee which doctors tried to flex. Returning to San Diego for a time, she went to Santa Barbara in November, then back to Coronado.

It was not until March, 1904, that Mother Amadeus returned to Montana.

On February 19, 1903, Miss Anita Rosecrans died of peritonitis in Helena. Her death saddened all at the Mission. Miss Rosecrans was a gifted musician—played the organ, piano and harp—and gave her services generously. For years she was the organist of the First Baptist Church in Helena. During her visits to her sister and brother-in-law, Mr. and Mrs. Joseph K. Toole, and after she made her home with them in Helena, she frequently came to St. Peter's to teach the novices harp and piano. Her first visit was on October 6, 1891, and from that time until her death in 1903 she made a number of visits, staying weeks at a time instructing the novices and young Sisters.

Anita's father was a convert to the Catholic faith, as was his brother who was ordained a priest in the diocese of Cincinnati. Later, Father Rosecrans became the first Bishop of Columbus, Ohio. He was an outstanding Bishop, led a humble life, and gave all he had to the poor and needy.

Anita's sister, Lily, married Joseph K. Toole, a successful lawyer, who became Montana's first Governor. His son, the late Warren K. Toole, also a lawyer, lived in Great Falls, Montana.

A brother of Governor Toole owned a large ranch in the Sweetgrass Hills. He sent his daughter, Claudia, to school at St. Peter's in September, 1892. She later married Con Price who was a close friend of Charlie Russell, the cowboy artist. Claudia's father often visited her at St. Peter's.

On June 27 Bishop Brondel arrived for what was to be his last visit to the Mission. He told the Sisters the story of the destruction of the Belt Church by fire; "how the candlesticks close to the tabernacle melted and everything burned to ashes except the little tabernacle that enclosed the ciborium holding the sacred Hosts."

After High Mass a group was confirmed and in the afternoon the boarders gave their closing exercises. The following day the Indian girls presented "The Last of the Mohicans," and several orchestra numbers.

The graduates in 1903 were Mary Ellen McCormack, Marguerite Caffrey, and Josephine Blanche Sullivan. Their commencement exercises consisted of selections from Dante's "*Divina Commedia*," a scene from "Athalie" by Racine, and harp selections by Miss Marguerite Caffrey.

During the summer months the Sisters frequently took the children on picnics and camping trips to Sullivan Valley and Dearborn. On Saturday, August 15, Sisters Paula, Elizabeth, and Annunciata went out for the day with a group of Indian girls. There were two wagonloads of picnickers. They were late returning and about nine o'clock a thunderstorm broke.

"A few miles from the school where the road runs along the creek the neck yoke straps on the second wagon, in which Sister Annunciata and other Nuns and pupils were riding, broke as the horses gave a sudden jump and the tongue fell to the ground. The frightened horses plunged to one side, pulling the wagon to the edge of the embankment and then broke away and ran as the wagon with its load toppled over the embankment to the creek fifteen feet below. So sudden was the accident that no one had an opportunity to escape, and as the wagon went over the cliff it turned over and fell upon all within it, pinning all but the driver beneath it in the mud."

Of the Nuns, Sister Annunciata was the most severely injured, and of the girls, Katie Reed suffered a broken jaw. Dr. Longeway came from Great Falls the following day and took Sister Annunciata and Katie Reed to Columbus Hospital. Sister had to undergo an operation to have a kidney removed, and Katie had a broken jaw which took some time to heal. Sister Paula's arm had been badly sprained and she required hospitalization later.

A group of soliders who had spent the summer in Yellowstone National Park and were returning to Fort Assiniboine, paraded on the Mission grounds to the great delight of the Sisters and children.

Father Prudenz was appointed pastor at Dillon, Montana, and was replaced by Father Van der Broeck.

On November 3, 1903, the sad news reached the Mission of the death of the great missionary, Bishop Brondel. The saintly Bishop had been the devoted friend of the Ursulines from the first day they arrived in Miles City in 1884.

In March, 1904, Mother Amadeus returned to Montana, called there by the serious illness of Sister Aurelia Enright, at St. Paul's Mission. Sister Aurelia's sister, Sister Felicitas, met Mother Amadeus and accompanied her to the Mission on Fort Belknap Reservation. There Mother developed pneumonia and was in danger of death. Sister Mary Rose left St. Peter's to be with her and Dr. Irwin came from Great Falls to attend her. After her recovery she spent the remainder of the year visiting the various Montana missions.

The graduation, which was always important at St. Peter's, took place on June 21 with three graduates, Misses Valine Fisher, Ursula Moran and Mary Slominsky. Ursula Moran gave the Salutatory and Valine Fisher the Valedictory address. The program included musical selections and a scene in French from Corneille's "Tragedie Chrêtienne."

Mother Amadeus arranged a retreat at St. Xavier's on August 25, 1904, for the Nuns of that Mission and those from Miles City, St. Labré's and some from St. Ignatius. Reverend Louis Taelman, S.J., conducted the exercises. Sisters Agatha, Lutegarde and Amata came from Miles City; Mother Mary of the Angels, Sisters Tecla, Gertrude and Rita from St. Labré's; Mother Amadeus with Sisters Perpetua, Caecilia, and Marion from St. Ignatius. They all met in Billings, traveled to the Crow Agency and then on to the Mission. On the return trip they had to stay overnight in the back of the church, sleeping on the floor. Father Taelman spent the night in the depot. Mother returned with the Nuns to Miles City and on September 8 started out for St. Labré's by train to Forsyth. She became ill and had to stop at Bean's ranch.

On the night of October 21, about eleven o'clock, ten exiled Ursulines from France arrived at Miles City. They were Mothers Marie Dosithée Leygonie, St. Angela Blake, St. Jean Baptiste Duchêne, Louise de Gonzague Boucheny, Marie Angele Cloître, Immaculate Conception Lecoq, Marie du Coeur de Jêsu, Mary Clémence Viguier, Sisters St. Euphrasia Frézal and St. Agnes Van Aerssen. Others came at various times to work on the missions. They included Mothers M. Joseph Guimard, Antonia Charpenay, Coeur de Marie Guienne, Eugénie Godefroy, Mary Clare Benoit, Gabriel Gonin, Agnes Altier, Francois d'Assise Baillet and Sister St. John of the Cross Fort. Nine died in Montana, and ten returned to France.

The Diocese of Helena, which included the entire state of Montana, was divided into two dioceses and two Bishops were named for the Sees of Helena and Great Falls. St. Peter's lay in that of Great Falls. Matthias Clement Lenihan was consecrated in Dubuque, Iowa, on September 21, 1904, for the Great Falls diocese and was installed on October 9 of the following month in his Episcopal See.[5]

There were no graduates from St. Peter's in 1907. Storms and floods kept many from attending the closing. The girls gave the usual musical selections and a section from Corneille's "Polyeucte." The Indian girls presented an operetta, "Laila."

In January, 1908, fire completely destroyed the boys' house and the Indian girls' seminary at St. Peter's. Flames poured from the roof of the boys' house which had been the

196

first stone building erected at the Mission. The Sisters and men carried out the bedding and Chapel furnishings while the priest removed the Blessed Sacrament. Sister Sebastian, a bedridden invalid, was taken temporarily to the Church Sacristy and later to the main building across the road. The destroyed building was constructed of stone but there was no means to save it. Sparks ignited a haystack and burned the cow sheds. That night the priest slept in the parlor, the boys in the music room and the Indian girls in the washhouse. The boys' school was closed and pupils sent home. Those who had no homes were sent to St. Ignatius Mission. The Indian girls were moved back to the main building which they had occupied prior to the closing of the Jesuit school.

The Hauser Dam gave way on April 15, causing floods in the area. Continuous rains in June increased the hazards so that the trains were halted.

The closing program in June, 1908, featured one graduate, Miss Elizabeth O'Neil. Nora Moran was married to Mr. Walsh in the old Mission Church and the Nuns served the wedding breakfast to the family in the Convent.

Travel was always a problem. One day Mother Perpetua, Sisters Lutegarde, Louis and Dolorosa left for Anaconda in the lumber wagon. As they jogged along the two Sisters Louis and Dolorosa fell asleep and rolled out. Sister Dolorosa was badly cut and had to be taken to a doctor for treatment.

Father Daniel Dineen, recently ordained, was appointed pastor and chaplain on January 6. At the same time, two lay teachers, Miss C. J. Moore and Miss Helen Pickering were hired. Miss Moore was a normal instructor and a help in training the young Sisters.

January 18, 1909, marked an important event for the Nuns. It was the twenty-fifth anniversary of the arrival of the Ursulines in Montana. Mother Amadeus presided over the celebration in Miles City with Mother Francis Seibert, one of the original group of missionaries.

The three Menager girls, Henrietta, Ann Marie and Mary Louise, arrived at the Mission. Two entered the Ursuline Order: Henrietta became Mother Loyola and Ann Marie, Mother Mary of the Incarnation. Later, Baby Loretta Lauterbach entered the Academy. She, too, entered the Order some years later. Recruitment during the early 1900's

197

came in large part from the West in contrast to the early groups who came from the Eastern part of the United States. When the Provincial Novitiate was established at Middletown, New York, in 1906, the postulants were sent there for the two years novitiate training. The first western novice to be professed there was Sister Stella Driscoll in September of that year. Sisters Divine Heart Cuff, Imelda Hanratty and Petronilla Seilnacht entered the Order in 1907; Sister Augustine Cuff in 1908; Sisters Loyola Menager, Bernadette and Emmanuel Adams, and Immaculata McLaughlin in 1909; Sisters Helen McVey and Vincent Sweeney in 1910; Sisters Mary of the Incarnation and Stanislaus McDonald in 1911, and Sisters Raphael Schweda, Patrick Crowley and Benedicta Callan in 1912.

Plans were made in 1910 to move the Academy to Great Falls. St. Peter's was not of easy access and a school in the city would attract day students as well as boarding students. The Sisters owned a half block in the heart of the city between Eighth and Ninth Streets on Second Avenue North, but Bishop Lenihan advised building farther out.

John D. Ryan was approached, relative to securing another site. John Morony, president of the Townsite Company, donated a block in Boston Heights for the new school. Since this site was farther from the populated area than desired, an exchange was made. Mr. Morony offered any two city blocks he owned. The final selection was made of two blocks on the south side of Central Avenue between Twenty-third and Twenty-fifth Streets. Later the Sisters exchanged the property on Second Avenue North in the 800 block for two blocks between First and Second Avenue South abutting the Central Avenue site.

George H. Shanley was selected as architect for the new building. The original plans called for a much smaller building of two and a half stories with dormer windows. This did not satisfy all the demands of a modern boarding and day school, so changes were made. The contract was awarded to H. S. Leigland of the firm of Leigland, Kleppe and Company of Glasgow, Montana.

The cornerstone was laid by Bishop Matthias Lenihan on September 17, 1911. Several came from St. Peter's for the ceremony: Father Purcell, his mother, Mother Francis Seibert, the Superior; Mothers Perpetua, Caecelia, Agnes, Annunciata, Margaret, Eulalia, Thomas, Berchmans, Aloysius and Redempta. Mothers Xavier and Loretta came from Anaconda and Mother Theresa and Sister Francis from Holy Family Mission near Browning.

The building was financed by $80,000 in bonds obtained from Belgium through the First National Bank in Great Falls and bankers in Salt Lake City, Utah. The finished building was turned over to the Nuns on July 3, 1912. On July 6 ten wagonloads of furniture left St. Peter's to fill the first carload sent to Great Falls. The second carload was shipped on July 19. Several Sisters, among them Mothers Loyola Menager, and Benedicta Callan, went to live in the unfurnished building to unpack and arrange the furnishings.

The transfer of the Motherhouse from St. Peter's to Great Falls occurred on July 24 when the Superior, Mother Francis, with Mothers Aloysius, Agnes, Annunciata and Berchmans took up residence in the new Academy. From that day the Mission of St. Peter continued as an Indian School for girls dependent on the house in Great Falls.

The Academy opened in Great Falls on September 3 with Mother Xavier Gavigan as Principal. Mother Lutegarde Jones became Superior of St. Peter's and Reverend Thomas Hennessy the Chaplain and Pastor.

[1] Mary Magdalen Bellasis, O.S.U., *Toward Unity*, adapted from the French of Marie Vianney Boschet, O.S.U. (Exeter, England: Catholic Records Press, 1952), pp. 212-213

[2] *Letter in the Annals*, vol. 5, p. 46

[3] *Annals*, St. Peter's, vol. 5.

[4] A narrow-gauge railroad had been built from Lethbridge to Johnston, a station in West Great Falls. Oldtimers called it the "Turkey Trail." It is said that one day a strong wind blew the train right off the track.

[5] *Great Falls Tribune*, October 9, 1904.

CHAPTER 10

Eyes on the North Star

Mother Amadeus (Sarah Dunne) was born in Akron, Ohio, on July 2, 1846. Her father, John Dunne, was from County Leinster, Ireland. He came to Canada in 1820 and thence to the United States; first to New York where he married Eleanore Dunne in Rochester in 1834. The family moved to the Western Reserve in Northern Ohio two years later. There were four children, Edmund, Sarah who died in her second year, John Joseph, Mary Ellen, and Sarah Therese who later became Mother Amadeus.

When Sarah was still a small child her father and older brother went to California. They were followed by the mother in 1856 and the two little girls were sent to the Ursuline boarding school in Cleveland. There the Dunnes formed a lasting friendship with the two Warner girls, Josie and Mary. Josie later married Sarah Dunne's brother, and Mary entered the Ursuline Order in Toledo, becoming Sister Annunciation.

When Sarah finished high school she applied for entrance at the Ursuline Convent in Toledo while Mary entered in Cleveland. Sarah received the cap of a postulant on December 12, 1861, and on September 2 of the following year she was accepted as a novice and took the name Amadeus, after that of the first Bishop of Cleveland, Bishop Amadeus Rappe. Her sister was known as Mother Mary of the Angels and became a gifted musician.

Two years later Sister Amadeus pronounced her vows. The superior of the Toledo Convent came for the occasion and brought with her Sister Mary of the Angels. When Mother Alphonsus, superior of the convent in Toledo, died in 1874, Sister Amadeus was elected to succeed her. In that office she served two terms of three years each, and the became Mistress of Novices.

On October 20, 1883, when Bishop Gilmore published a letter in the *Catholic Universe*, asking for volunteers to go to Montana to help teach the Cheyenne Indians, thirty Sisters volunteered. Sister Amadeus was among them. From the thirty, six were chosen, including Mother Amadeus as superior of the group.

For many years Mother Amadeus had dreamed of an Order of native Indian Sisters who would help in the apostolic work among their own people. As early as October 18, 1896, when she sent Sister Paula to take charge of St. Labré's Mission, she sent with her Mary Wallace as a helper and teacher. Mary Wallace was a Piegan Indian who came to the school at St. Peter's April 1, 1888, at the age of ten years. Since then she had progressed in her studies and was able to assist the Sisters.

Another promising subject was Watzinitha, a Gros Ventre, who was especially gifted and had been at the Mission since June 5, 1886, when she was eight years old. Mother Amadeus brought her to St. Labré's where she first intended to open the novitiate for these Sisters. On May 24, 1898, Mother left there with the two girls and took them to St. Ignatius where they received the cap on June 17, 1898. There the postulants were under the spiritual direction of Reverend Father Cocehi, S.J.

In September, 1900, Mary Wallace, then Sister Amadeus, was at St. Peter's helping to teach the Cheyenne group.

Mechtilde, a Gros Ventre, asked to be a postulant, but was ill. However, Mother Amadeus gave her the cap on January 27, 1899 and she lived just two weeks.

Ida Sanborn, another Gros Ventre, came to St. Peter's at the age of six years on May 13, 1888. She entered as a postulant later, but left on August 5, 1901, with a companion postulant of the same tribe named Mary Lucy.

The only one of the group to be professed was Watzinitha, or Sister Immaculata. She returned ill from St. Ignatius on October 17, 1898, and was permitted to make her vows on December 18, 1901. Sister was too ill to leave the infirmary, so a temporary altar was erected there. The Nuns formed a procession for the ceremony, each with a lighted taper.

Father Pudenz, the chaplain, presided at the simple but beautiful rites. Parts were sung as in the regular profession ceremony of the Ursulines. Sister, too weak to sing, said her part in Latin. A few days later, on December 30, the dear novice, the first and last professed of the native group, died at 11:45 P.M.

On August 6, 1905, the foundress of the Montana Ursuline Missions accompanied the first Alaska-bound Missionaries to Seattle: Mother Laurentia Walsh, Sister Claver Driscoll, and Sister Dosithée Leygonie. These Ursuline missionaries settled at the Jesuit Mission of Akulurak on the Yukon delta. Mother Amadeus returned to Montana for a short time, then with Mother Amata she sailed for Rome where she remained until the following year.

In April, 1906, the Sisters in Montana received the welcome news that Mother Amadeus had been appointed the first Provincial of the Northern Province of the United States. In May, the following month, Mother General St. Julian arrived in the United States, accompanied by Mother Amadeus, to make a visitation of all the Ursuline Convents belonging to the Roman Union. They went first to St. Peter's where an election was held to secure a new Superior for the Montana houses. Mother Francis Seibert was elected.

Reverend Mother St. Julian and Mother Amadeus, after visiting the Montana missions, went to New York where they selected the site at Middletown for a novitiate in August, 1906. Henceforth the novices from Montana would go there for their training. Mother Amadeus was selected the following year as a delegate to the General Chapter in Rome.

In September, 1908, Mother was again at St. Peter's on her way to Alaska with Mother Angela Lincoln, Mother de Merici Shebel, Mother Bartholomew and Sister Margaret Mary. She wrote of the trip to Father Lindesmith:

Well, my dear friend, my journey to and from Alaska was a perilous one. I found myself in Unimak Pass, between the beetling crags on the very day of the equinoctial storms. Our short little ship fought hard with the frantic waves and winds of the Bering Sea, and we were obliged to keep up under a full head of steam merely not to be driven back.

At length, on September 24th, Our Lady of Mercy Day, we crossed the golden bar of Nome where our gallant ship stopped for a few hours to unload passengers and freight...when we put out to sea again to cross Norton Sound to St. Michael's, the wild grandeur of the scene exceeded all that the most fervid imagination could paint.

The Commanding Officer of the Fort, with true American courtesy, gave us a home free of rent for two years.

When the outgoing ship bore me from St. Michael on Oct. 15th, I had the consolation of opening our little convent, "St. Ursula by the Sea" and of leaving there three of my brave Nuns, auxiliaries to the three valiant ones already at Akulurak.[1]

On January 18, 1909, the twenty-fifth anniversary of the coming of the Ursulines to Montana was commemorated. A fitting celebration was prepared in Miles City, over which the foundress presided.

In May of that year, Mother Irene Gill was appointed Provincial to replace Mother Amadeus. She again went to Rome in 1910 as a delegate to the third General Chapter. On her return, she went directly to Alaska, accompanied by Mother Angela Lincoln and Mother Alphonsus of Frontenac, Minnesota. She always spoke of this trip as the journey "from Rome to Nome."

After several months at St. Michael's, she went to Akulurak, There she received word from Bishop Crimont, asking for Sisters for a convent at Valdez. She appointed Mother Mary of the Angels Carrol from St. Peter's as Superior and sent her with Sister Helen of Toledo and two postulants in May, 1912, to make the foundation there.[2] In order to reach Valdez it was necessary for Mother Amadeus to return to Seattle from Akulurak and take a boat direct to Valdez. After a stay at Valdez, she left Alaska to recruit subjects for the Alaskan Missions and visited in Spokane in the summer of 1913.

When the Mother Vicar, Marguerite, with her companion, Mother Evangelista, came to the United States in 1914, Mother Amadeus met them in Great Falls and went with them to Seattle to arrange for a novitiate for the Alaskan Missions. She wrote from Seattle:

Our Novitiate is now opened in a very small eight-room rented house for $30.00 per month.

On the very day of my Golden Jubilee, August 23rd, it was given me to renew my vows, surrounded by the first Alaskan Novices and one Ursuline from the dear old Toledo home, and three Ursulines from Montana. And on that day, too, did I send two more professed Nuns up to Northern Alaska. It seemed as though my joy must be complete.[3]

The two Nuns mentioned were Mother Coeur de Marie Thoissey from France and Sister Rose from Toledo. Sister Immaculata McLaughlin, who had volunteered for the Alaskan Missions, accompanied Mother Coeur de Marie from Great Falls but was detained in Seattle to teach in a parochial school.

The novitiate soon proved unsuitable and a larger building was secured at St. Helen's Place. This site became a source of trouble with the neighbors who objected to this institution in a residential area. The difficulty and dispute was finally settled in favor of the Sisters.

In August, 1918, Mother Amadeus and her companion left Valdez on the *Victoria* for St. Michael's. On board was Bishop Crimont, S.J. From St. Michael's they traveled to St. Mary's at Akulurak, then up the Yukon to Holy Cross Mission. From there a steamer took the party down the river on to St. Michael's. A disastrous fire destroyed the convent at St. Michael's on December 9, leaving them without necessities. The Quartermaster at the Fort furnished them with blankets and shelter at the U.S. Army Post. The foundress returned to Seattle in 1919 in a dying condition.[4]

During the summer a school for orphans was opened at Pilgrim Springs near Nome. Mother Theresa of St. Joseph, Mother Mary of the Holy Name and Sister Tecla went from Rome to Seattle where they were joined by Sister Irene and Sister Berchmans for the trip North.

At this time, Mother Amadeus was near death, and on

November 10, 1919, she passed to eternity. Her life was heroic; nothing ever deterred her when she decided to carry on her charity to the Indian and Eskimo. Her body was brought to St. Ignatius where she was buried in the beautiful Flathead Valley.

[1] *Letter*, Mother Amadeus to Father Lindesmith, Middletown, New York, December 15, 1908. Catholic University Archives, Washington, D.C.

[2] Clotilde Angela McBride, *The Ursulines of the West*, pp. 67-68. Also *Ursuline Annals*, St. Peter's.

[3] *Letter*, Mother Amadeus to Father Lindesmith, Dec. 18, 1914. Seattle, Washington.

[4] Mother Angela Lincoln, *Life of Reverend Mother Amadeus of the Heart of Jesus*, pp. 198-205.

EPILOGUE

The first Mission in Montana, St. Labré's, suffered a disaster on the 12th of January, 1917, when fire completely destroyed the "White House," the convent and school. Bishop Lenihan always loved this Mission and was proud of the valorous missionaries who labored there. He loved to tell the story of his determination to keep the Mission operating. Mother Thomas, the Superior at the time, wired the Bishop that the convent and school were leveled to the ground and asked what they should do. The answer came back, "Hold the fort." The sacristy became the kitchen "de luxe," the Sisters and children slept in the choir loft while the nave was reserved for the school.[1] New buildings were soon erected and today the mission florishes.

It was not long until the work at St. Peter's ended. On the morning of November 12, 1918, at 3:00 A.M., fire was discovered on the main floor under the children's dormitory in the large stone convent and school. There were seven Sisters and forty-two children in the building at the time. All were taken out safely but little was saved of the furnishings. The neighbors came and fought the flames but the battle was useless. The building was ablaze and no adequate system was available to save it.

Today at St. Peter's heaps of rubble mark the location of the schools. The little log Church still stands at one end of the Mission grounds and at the other, the "Opera House," symbolic of the attempt to bring Christianity and culture into the wilderness.

[1] *Ursuline Annals.*

APPENDIX A

FIRST PUPILS AT URSULINE ACADEMY, ST. PETER'S MISSION, MONTANA

1885

Mollie Lewis, daughter of Ed Lewis
Martha and Annie Brown, daughters of John Brown
Julie Wiegand, daughter of George Wiegand
Louise and Millie Ford, daughters of Sam Ford
Alice, Rose, and Laura Aubrey, daughters of Charles Aubrey

1886

Agnes and Babe Moran, daughters of Mr. H. Moran
Clara Davis, daughter of Clara Davis
Louisa Miller, daughter of Mrs. H. Miller
Katie Hines, daughter of John Hines
Mary Reed, daughter of Mrs. Margaret Reed (Pat Connelly)
Katie Pambrun, daughter of A. Pambrun

1887

Mamie Furman, daughter of Coby Furman
Sadie Smith, daughter of George V. Smith
Marguerite Connelly, daughter of George V. Smith
Anna Quigley, daughter of J.R. Quigley
Lily Conrad, daughter of Mrs. J.D. Conrad
Alice Burd, daughter of S.C. Burd
Miss Curran, daughter of Mrs. M. Curran
R. Ferris, daughter of Mrs. J. Hensley

Katie Tully, daughter of T. J. Tully
Mary and Rose Furman, daughters of Coby Furman
Anna and Susan Kennelly, daughters of Mrs. Anna Kennelly
Flora Bergeron, daughter of Mrs. Louise Bergeron
Mary Lenihan, daughter of Mrs. Mary Lenihan
Etta and Clara Shanks, daughters of Mrs. W. B. Shanks
Edith and Adele Moore, daughter of Mrs. C. B. Shields
Lizzie Tully, daughter of T.J. Tully
Mary Juneau, daughter of Andrew O'Connor
Jeannie Price, daughter of Mrs. Price French
Katie Mahoney, daughter of Mrs. D. Mahoney
Gracie Chene, daughter of Mrs. Gabriel Chene
Lida Ousley, daughter of Mrs. Gabriel Chene
Dora Keiley
Nellie Rand, daughter of Moses Morris
Katie and Agnes Finnegan, daughters of Mrs. P. Finnegan
Miss Clark, daughter of I. N. Clark

1889

Alice Rand, daughter of Moses Morris
Frankie Porter, daughter of Alexander Porter
R. and F. Schaeffer, daughters of Peter Schaeffer

ENROLLMENT
1885 - 1905

| | | Indian | |
		Boys	Girls
1885	March 7, 1885 to July 1, 1886	15	14
1886	July 1, 1886 to July 1, 1887	25	35
1887	July 1, 1887 to July 1, 1888	23	26
1888	July 1, 1888 to July 1, 1889	31	42
1889	July 1, 1889 to July 1, 1890	42	52
1890	July 1, 1890 to July 1, 1891	85	113
1891	July 1, 1891 to July 1, 1892	96	117
1892	July 1, 1892 to July 1, 1893	105	111
1893	July 1, 1893 to July 1, 1894	100	114
1894	July 1, 1894 to July 1, 1895	100	118
1895	July 1, 1895 to July 1, 1896	85	116
1896	July 1, 1896 to July 1, 1897		80
1897	July 1, 1897 to July 1, 1898		98
1898	July 1, 1898 to July 1, 1899		106
1899	July 1, 1899 to July 1, 1900		108
1900	July 1, 1900 to July 1, 1901	8	118
1901	July 1, 1901 to July 1, 1902	6	105
1902	July 1, 1902 to July 1, 1903	6	103
1903	July 1, 1903 to July 1, 1904	8	100
1904	July 1, 1904 to July 1, 1905	5	82

BIBLIOGRAPHY

Primary Sources

Abair, Sister St. Angela: *A Mustard Seed in Montana*, Recollections of the First Indian Mission in Montana, Toledo, 1938.

Bobbitt, J.N.: *The Sun River Stampede of 1866.* (Ms.) Montana Historical Library. Helena, September 1923.

Bradley, Lieut. J. H.: "Account of the St. Peter's Mission, Montana." *Contributions to the Historical Society of Montana*, Vol. 9, pp. 315-316, 1923. "Sun River Stampede 1860." *Contributions of the Historical Society of Montana*, Vol. 9, pp. 251-252, 1923.

Brondel, Rt. Rev. John B.: Letters referring to St. Peter's Mission—Feb. 17, 1884 - July 3, 1894. (Ms) Ursuline Archives.

Cataldo, S.J., Rev. Joseph: *Letter* dated April 14, 1890—St. Peter's Mission. (Ms.) Ursuline Archives.

Chittenden, Hiram Martin and Richardson, Alfred Talbot: *Life, Letters and Travels of Father Pierre-Jean De Smet, S. J. 1801-1873.* 4 Vols. New York, F. P. Harper, 1905.

Choteau, Charles P.: *Steamboat Journey from St. Louis to Fort Benton.* (Ms.) Montana Historical Library. His report to the Secretary of War of a steamboat journey from St. Louis to Fort Benton, 1859.

Cox, Ross: *Adventurer on the Columbia River* including the Narrative of a Residence of six years on the Western side of the Rocky Mountains among various tribes of Indians hitherto unknown together with a Journey Across the American Continent. 2 Vols. London, Henry Colburn and Richard Bently 1831 (original edition).

211

Damiani, S. J., Rev. Joseph: *Letter* dated Aug. 12, 1889—St. Paul's Mission (Ms.) Ursuline Archives.

De Camp, Ralph: Roy P. Johnson Collection. *Notes* and *Letters* relating to Ralph de Camp in Assumption Abbey Archives, Richardton, North Dakota.

De Smet, S.J., Rev. Pierre Jean: *Cinquante Nouvelles Lettres du R. P. DeSmet. Paris, 1858.*

—— *New Indian Sketches.* New York, 1904. (Contains catechism in Indian)

—— *Oregon Missions and Travels over the Rocky Mountains in 1845-1846.* New York, 1847.

—— *Western Missions and Missionaries: A Series of Letters.* New York, P. J. Kenedy, 1859.

Dictionary of the Flathead Indian Language, Compiled by the missionaries of the Society of Jesus. 2 Vols. St. Igantius, Mont. 1877-9. Part 1. Kalispell—English; Part 2. English—Kalispell.

Dunne, Mother Amadeus: *Letters* to Father E.J.W. Lindesmith. (Ms.) Archives Catholic University of America. Washington, D.C.

Fisk Expedition: Expedition from Fort Abercrombie to Fort Benton 1862. House of Representatives 37th Congress 3rd Session.

Gilmore, Rt. Rev. Richard: *Letters* dated Dec. 19, 1883, April 7, 1883, April 6, 1884, June 16, 1884, July 28, 1884, January 13, 1889. Cleveland. (MS.) Ursuline Archives.

Giorda, S. J., Rev. Joseph: *Letter to M. Gad E. Upson.* (Ms.) Archives Indian Bureau, Washington, D.C. 1864.

Hauser, S. J., Rev. Theo.: *Letter* dated May 5, 1884. Toledo. (Ms.) Ursuline Archives.

Kahlehat: News Letters No. 1-4, 1914-1919. Ursuline Archives.

Larpenteur, Charles: *Forty Years a Fur Trader on the Upper Missouri: the personal narrative of Charles Larpenteur 1833-1872.* ed. Elliott Coues, New York, F. P. Harper, 1898.

Lindesmith, E.: Diaries. March 1880—July, 1891. (9 diaries) (Ms.) Archives Catholic University of America, Washington, D.C.

—— Letters, notes and papers. (Ms.) Archives, Catholic

University of America. His personal copy of Notes and annotation in Palladino, *Indian and White in the Northwest*. Ursuline Archives, Great Falls, Montana.

Owen, Major John: *The Journals and Letters of Major John Owen, Pioneer of the Northwest 1850-1881*, embracing his purchase of St. Mary's Mission: the building of Fort Owen; his travels; his relations with the Indians; his work for the Government; and his activities as a western empire builder for twenty years. Transcribed and edited from the manuscripts in the Montana Historical Society and the Collection of W.R. Con, esq. by Seymour Dunbar; and with notes to Owen's texts by Paul C. Phillips. 2 Vols. New York, E. Eberstadt Co., 1927. (Contains references to missionaries.)

Point, S. J., Rev. Nicholas: *A journey in a Barge on the Missouri from the Fort of the Blackfeet (Lewis) to that of the Assiniboines (Union)*, Particulars Edifying or Curious, translated from the French by Paul A. Barrette, Department of Modern Language, St. Louis University. (Splendid description of Fort Lewis.)

—— *Wilderness Kingdom:* Indian Life in the Rocky Mountains 1840-1847. The Journals and Paintings of Nicholas Point, S. J., translated and introduced by Joseph P. Donnelly, S. J. New York, Holt, Rinehart and Winston, 1967.

Ravalli, S. J., Rev. Anthony: *Letter of Father Ravalli to Miss Narcissa Caldwell*, June 16, 1884. (Ms.) Historical Library, Helena.

—— *Manuscript in Latin.* Presented by Rev. Chas. F. Richardson of Great Falls, Mont., Dec. 12, 1905.

Report of the Commissioner of Indian Affairs for the Year 1863. Washington: Government Printing Office 1867.

Report of the Joint Special Committee appointed under Joint Resolution of March 3, 1865 with an appendix. Washington Government Printing Office 1867.

Report of the Commissioner of Indian Affairs for the Year 1866. Washington: Government Printing Office 1866.

Report of Indian Affairs by the Acting Commissioner for the Year 1867. Washington: Government Printing Office 1868.

Roe, Frances M. A. *Army Letters from an Officer's Wife 1871—1888.* New York and London, D. Appleton & Co., 1909.

Roehm, Marjorie Catlin: *The Letters of George Catlin and His Family.* A Chronicle of the American West. Berkeley and Los Angeles, University of California Press, 1966.

Sacred Heart, Sister: *A History of the Northern Cheyenne.* (Ms.) Ursuline Archieves, Great Falls, 1885.

Seghers, Most Rev. Charles John: Archbishop of Oregon City and Administrator Apostolic of the Vicariate of Idaho—To the Clergy, both secular and regular, the Religious communities, and the Faithful of the Western Part of Montana, 1883. (Pastoral.)

Sister Sainte Scholastique: *Letter* (sections). (Ms.) Ursuline Archives, Great Falls, Montana, 1918.

Stuart, Granville: *Forty Years on the Frontier* as seen in the journals and reminiscences of Granville Stuart, goldminer, trader, merchant, rancher and politician Ed. by Paul C. Phillips. 2 Vols., Cleveland, The Arthur H. Clark Co.

Tuttle, Rev. D. S.: *Reminiscences of a Missionary Bishop.* New York, D. Whitaker, 1906.

Uhlenbeck, C. C.: *A New Series of Blackfoot Texts from the Southern Piegan Blackfoot Reservation, Teton County, Montana.* Amsterdam, 1912.

Ursulines: Annals of St. Peter's Mission 1891—1912. 5 Vols. (Vol. 1 missing) (Ms.) Ursuline Archives.

—— Annals of St. Labre's Mission 1896—1916. 3 Vols. (not continuous) (Ms.) Ursuline Archives.

Letters of Ursuline Missionaries. (Ms.) Ursuline Archives, Toledo, Ohio. Copies Archives, Great Falls, Montana.

Wyeth, Nathaniel J.: *Correspondence and Journal of Captain Nathaniel J. Wyeth*, 1831—6. Ed. by F. Young, Eugene, Oregon, University Press, 1899.

Secondary Sources

American Catholic Historical Society. Vol. 1, 1884—1886. Philadelphia.

Bancroft, Hubert Howe: *History of the Northwest Coast 1543—1800*. 2 Vols. San Francisco, A. L. Bancroft & Co., 1884.

— *History of Oregon 1834—1848*. 2 Vols. San Francisco, The History Company, 1886.

— *History of Washington, Idaho and Montana 1845—1889* San Francisco 1896.

Bellasis, O.S.U. Mary Magdelene: *Toward Unity*. Vol. 1. History of the Roman Union of the Order of Saint Ursula adapted from the French of Marie Vianney Boschet, O.S.U. Catholic Records Press Exeter, 1952.

Brown, Dee: *Bury My Heart at Wounded Knee*, an Indian History of the America West. New York, Holt, Rinehart & Winston, 1970.

Chittenden, Hiram Martin: *History of the Early Steamboat Navigation on the Missouri River*. Life and adventures of Joseph La Barge, pioneer navigator and Indian trader for fifty years, identified with the commerce of the Missouri Valley. 2 Vols. New York, F. P. Harper. 1903.

— *The American Fur Trade of the Far West*. 3 Vols. New York, Frances P. Harper, 1902.

Collections of the State Historical Society of North Dakota. 7 Vols.

Contributions to Historical Society of Montana. 10 Vols. Helena 1876-1930.

Curley, Edward P.: *Origin and Progress of the Catholic Church*. Helena 1927 (Reprint from Records of the American Catholic Historical Society, Philadelphia, March and June 1927.)

Davis, S. J., William L.: *A History of St. Ignatius Mission*, An Outpost of Catholic Culture on the Montana Frontier, Spokane, C. W. Hill Printing, Co., 1954.

Desière, Rev. P.: *A Life Sketch of Father De Ryckers*. (Ms.) Historical Library.

Dinsdale, T. J.: *Vigilantes of Montana, Virginia City, Montana*, T. E. Castle and C. W. Bank, 1921.

Duffy, S.B.S., Sister Consuela Marie: *Katharine Drexel*. A Biography. Philadelphia, The Peter Reilly Company, 1966.

Fuller, G. W.: *The Inland Empire of the Pacific Northwest*. A

History. Spokane, Denver, H. G. Linderman, 1928.

Garraghan, S. J., Rev. Gilbert J.: *Chapters in Frontier History*. Research studies in the making of the West. Milwaukee, Bruce Pub. Co., 1934.

—— *The Jesuits of the Middle United States*. 3 Vols. New York, America Press, 1938.——

—— *Trans-Mississippi West*. Nicholas Point, Jesuit Missionary in Montana of the Forties.

—— *Documents*. An Early Missouri River Journal. (Illinois Catholic Historical Publication.)

Great Falls Yesterday: Comprising a collection of biographies and reminiscences of early settlers. Edith Maxwell ed., Great Falls, Montana.

Grennell, George B.: *The Fighting Cheyennes*. Norman: University of Oklahoma Press, 1956.

Harrod, Howard L.: *Mission Among the Blackfeet*. Norman: University of Oklahoma Press, 1971.

Houek, George F., Rev.: *The Church in Northern Ohio and in the Diocese of Cleveland from 1749—1890*. Cleveland: Short and Forman, 1890.

Howard, Joseph Kinsey: *Montana High, Wide, and Handsome*. New Haven: Yale University Press, 1943.

—— *Strange Empire*. A Narrative of the Northwest. New York: William Morrow and Company, 1952.

Hughes, Katherine: *Father Lacomba, The Black Robe Voyageur*. New York, 1911.

John Francis, O.S.U., Sister: *The Broad Highway*. A History of the Ursuline Nuns, Cleveland, 1951.

Judson, Katherine B.: *Subject Index to the History of the Pacific Northwest and of Alaska* as found in the U.S. Government Documents. Congressional Series, in the American State Papers and in other Documents 1789—1881. Washington State Library, Olympia, 1913.

Jung, A. M.: *Jesuit Missions Among the American Tribes of the Rocky Mountain Indians*. Spokane: Gonzaga University, 1925.

LaVeille, E.: *Life of Father De Smet, S. J., (1801—1873)* trans. by Marian Lindsay. New York: P. J. Kenedy & Sons, 1915.

Lincoln, Mother Angela: *Life of Mother Amadeus of the Heart of Jesus: Foundress of Ursuline Missions of*

Montana and Alaska. New York: Paulist Press, 1923.

Long, James Larpenteur: *Land of Nakoda.* The story of the Assiniboine Indians. From the tales of Old Ones told to First Boy (James L. Long) with drawings by Fire Bear (William Standing) under the direction of the Writers' Program of the Works Projects Administration in the State of Montana. Helena State Pub. Co., 1942.

Mallet, Major Edmond: "The origin of the Flathead Mission of the Rocky Mountains." *American Catholic Historical Society.* Vol. 2, pp. 175—205.

Marquis, Thomas B.: *A Warrior Who Fought Custer.* Minneapolis, The Midwest Company, 1931.

McBride, Mother Clotilde: *Ursulines of the West.* Mt. Angel, Oregon, Mt. Angel Press, 1936.

McClintock, Walter: *The Old North Trail.* Boston and New York, Houghton, Mifflin Co., 1923.

Mildred, S.S.A., Sister Mary *The Apostle of Alaska.* Life of the Most Reverend Charles John Seghers. Trans. of Maurice De Baets', "Vie de Monseigneur Seghers". Paterson, N. J., St. Anthony Guild, 1943.

Murdock, George Peter: *Ethnographic Bibliography of North America.* New Haven, Yale University Press, 1941.

Oregon Historical Society Quarterly 30 Vols. 1900—1929, Portland

Palladino, S. J., Rev. Lawrence B.: *Anthony Ravalli, S. J., Forty Years a Missionary in the Rocky Mountains.*

— *Indian and White in the Northwest or a History of Catholicity in Montana,* with an introduction by Right Rev. John B. Brondel. First Bishop of Helena, Baltimore, 1894.

Progressive Men of Montana. Chicago

Ravalli, Rev. Anthony: Biographical sketch (clipping from the Missoulian, March 8, 1904).

Raymer, Robert George: *Montana, the Land and the People* Chicago, 1930.

Reilly, Louis W.: "Father Ravalli, Pioneer Indian Missionary." *The Catholic World,* April 1927.

Ronan, Peter: *Historical Sketch of the Flathead Indian Nation from the year 1813 to 1890.* Embracing the history of the establishment of St. Mary's Indian Mission in the Bitter Root Valley, Montana, with sketches of the missionary life of Father Ravalli and other early missionaries, wars of the Blackfeet and Flatheads and sketches of history, trapping and trading in the early days. Helena: Journal Publishing Co., 1890.

Sanders, Helen Fitzgerald: *History of Montana.* 3 Vols., Chicago. 1913.

—— *Trails through Western Woods.* New York & Seattle: The Alice Harriman Company, 1910.

Savage, A. H.: *Dogsled Apostles.* New York: Sheed & Ward, 1942.

Schoenberg, S. J., Wilfred P.: *A Chronicle of the Catholic History of the Pacific Northwest 1743—1960.* Portland: Catholic Sentinel Printing, 1962.

—— *Jesuits in Montana, 1840—1960.* Portland, 1960.

—— *Jesuit Mission Presses in the Pacific Northwest.* Portland, 1957.

Shea, John Gilmary: *Defenders of the Faith, the Church in the United States and Canada* with Portraits and Biographies of Her Archbishops and Bishops. New York: Office of Catholic Publications, 1891.

Sirango, Charles A.: *A Cowboy Detective.* A true story of twenty-two years with a world famous detective agency. New York, 1912.

—— *Riata and Spurs.* The story of a lifetime spent in the saddle as cowboy and detective. Cambridge: Riverside Press, 1927.

Stevens, Hazard: *Life of Isaac Ingals Stevens.* 2 Vols. Boston: Houghton, Mifflin & Co., 1900.

Stewart, Edgar I.: *Custer's Luck.* Norman: University of Oklahoma Press, 1955.

Swanton, John R.: *The Indian Tribes of North America.* Washington, D.C.: Smithsonian Instituion, Bureau of American Ethnology, Bulletin 145, U.S. Government Printing Office, 1953.

Ursulines of Brown County, Ohio: *A Member of the Community.* Fifty Years in Brown County Convent. Cincinnati: McDonald & Co., 1895.

Vaughn, Robert: *Then and Now or Thirty-six Years in the Rockies.* Personal Reminiscences of Some of the First Pioneers of the State of Montana. Minneapolis: Tribune Printing Co., 1900.

Waller, Brown: *Last of the Great Western Train Robbers.* New York: A. S. Barnes & Co., 1968.

Wissler, Clark: *The American Indian.* New York: Oxford University Press, 1938.

NEWSPAPERS

Fort Benton
    Benton Weekly Record
    Vo. 1 No. 1 (Feb. 1, 1975) to Vol. 9 No. 29 (May 10, 1884)
    River Press
        Vol. 1 No. 1 (Oct. 27, 1885)

Helena
    Daily Montana News
        Vol. 1 No. 31 (Sept. 1, 1875) to Vol. 2 No. 32 (Feb. 8, 1876)
    Daily Montanian
        Vol. 1 No. 33 (Feb. 10, 1885) to Vol. 1 No. 34 (Feb. 11, 1885)
    Helena Daily Record
        Vol. 1 No. 1 (Sept. 7, 1888) to Vol. 1 No. 163 (March 17, 1889)
    The Helena Era (Weekly)
        Vol. 1 No. 1 (June 27, 1883) to Vol. 1 No. 12 (Oct. 13, 1883)
    The Helena Herald
        Vol. No. 1 (Nov. 15, 1866) to Vol. 34 No. 4 (Dec. 27, 1902)
    The Helena Independent
        Vol. 1 (Sept. 24, 1872) Vol. 5 No. 8 *(July 1, 1874)*
    Montana News Letter
        Vol. 1 No. 5 (March 21, 1889) No. 6 (April 1, 1889) No. 8 (April 3, 1889) No. 11 (May 8, 1889)
    The Tri-Weekly Republican
        Vol. 1 No. 5 (Sept. 25, 1864) to No. 31 (July 26, 1866)
    Helena Weekly Herald
Miles City

219

Daily Courier
 Vol. 1 No. 4 (Oct. 18, 1888) to Vol. 4 No. 27 (Nov. 10, 1894)
Daily Record
 Vol. 1 No. 30 (Sept. 13, 1884) to Vol. 1 No. 70 (Oct. 30, 1884)
Miles City Daily Press
 Vol. 1 No. 3 (July 27, 1883) to Vol. 2 No. 84 (Sept. 19, 1883)
Stockgrowers' Journal
 Vol. 9 No. 32 (May 6, 1898)—(Dec. 27, 1916)
The Yellowstone Journal
 Vol. 1 No. 6 (Aug. 28, 1879)—(Jan. 15, 1918)
Sun River
 Vol. 1 No. 1 (Feb. 4, 1884) to Vol. 2 No. 11 (April 3, 1885)
The Rising Sun
 Vol. 1 No. 1 (Aug. 13, 1885) to Vol. 12 No. 19 (Dec. 23, 1896)

Virginia City
Montana Post
 Vol. 1 No. 1 (Aug. 27, 1864) to Vol. 5 No. 11 (June 11, 1869)